THE TRUE STORY OF

THERESA

THE MOST BEAUTIFUL ROSE

To Jeanine

Thank you for walking 4 Theresa's memory each year

Love
Nancy

Oct 15, 2010.

THE TRUE STORY OF

THERESA

THE MOST BEAUTIFUL ROSE

By

Nancy M. Moore

Copyright © 1997, 2000 by Nancy M. Moore

All rights reserved.
No part of this book may be reproduced, restored in a retrieval system, or transmitted by means, electronic, mechanical, photocopying, recording, or otherwise, without written consent from the author.

ISBN: 1-58721-992-1

Library of Congress Number: Txu 815-517

1stBooks - rev. 8/22/00

ABOUT THE BOOK

Who was Theresa? She was our daughter. She was a gift, a joy. She was a devoted wife, a young mother, and an extraordinary individual. This book will give you a glimpse into her personal life, family life, and her struggle to fight a devastating killer—breast cancer.

She was a person with exceptional human values, and extreme determination. She possessed immeasurable courage. Her spirit, energy and religious faith were her sources of strength.

Everyone should be blessed with knowing at least one person like Theresa in his or her own lifetime. Now is your time and opportunity to experience such an individual.

Trust me, she will truly endear you and revitalize your appreciation of life, family and relationships.

This writing can help all families to work harder at listening and loving. Perhaps in some small way, her story will be a source of solace and sustenance to those who come to know her through this tribute.

ACKNOWLEDGEMENTS

It is with deep gratitude that I acknowledge the following individuals, medical facilities, media sources, and organizations that played such an important part inTheresa's life.

To Theresa's cousin, Cynthia Moore Dowling, who introduced me to a computer, I am ever grateful. To Diane Kelleher, who educated me in the use of it, I thank for the assistance and patience in helping me to keep her best friend's memory alive. I also appreciate Diane's near daily phone calls since March 27, 1997. Surely she is fulfilling Theresa's request.

A special thanks to the following for allowing me to include them by name in my book:

John Dempsey Hospital, University of Connecticut Campus, Farmington, Connecticut.

Rochester General Hospital, Portland Avenue, Rochester, New York.

Ann Sass, RN, and Clinical Trial Contact Person, Rochester General Hospital Cancer Center, Rochester, New York.

Larry Camerlin, President of Angel Flight New England, which is now located at the Lawrence Municipal Airport, Andover, Massachusetts.

Producer Tim Gorin and Dateline NBC, New York, New York.

Hartford Courant, Hartford, Connecticut.

Democrat Chronicle Times, Rochester, New York.

Chronicle of WCVB TV, Channel 5, Boston, Massachusetts.

The American Cancer Society.

To my editor, Jerie Larsen, who felt such deep emotion about the book, we could never meet and discuss it without tears.

To Gail Swedberg, of GSM Design, Portsmouth, New Hampshire, for the cover design.

To my dear husband, Tom, for understanding my need to do the book and for being so patient and supportive while I spent countless hours, first on the hand-written manuscript, and then with my graduation to the computer which required so much of my time. I will forever remember his leaning over my shoulder and asking me, "How are you doing?" The fact is that I couldn't have done it without him. He helped me to bring so many precious memories to the surface and magnified for me all that we have been blessed with in our lives together.

DEDICATION

I dedicate this book to our dear granddaughter, Madison Marie. I felt compelled to write it to share with her, and all who might read it, the qualities and beauty of her mother, Theresa.

It is fitting that the events in the life of this beautiful young woman be written so that she might be appreciated for the unique human being she was.

Theresa's life was a gift to all that knew her and perhaps to some that didn't.

I love her still; I'll love her always.

PREFACE

What I wish to convey to the readers of this book is the importance of having hope, faith, optimism, and courage.

In more and more instances, because of all the advances in medical research, illnesses which once had very poor prognoses are now curable or are able to be better managed, thus, affording a finer quality of life for many individuals.

I think that we must look at each tomorrow as being a day closer to better controlling or eradicating serious diseases. We must all live with that hope, for there is always a new day dawning.

FOREWORD

As a teen-ager my daughter, Theresa, used to say to me, "Mom, someday you have to write a book."

As a woman my daughter, Theresa, used to say to me, "Mom, someday you have to write a book."

I am so very saddened to have had the occasion to write this book. However, as I wrote it, it became such a strong connection to my beloved Theresa. It was as if she were with me, guiding me through the journey that I began on March 29, 1997, and completed on July 27, 1997.

When this book was finished, I had a feeling of great fulfillment, and yet I felt such a tremendous emptiness. It seemed as if we were parting again. It was a realization that I must let it go, as I had to let her go.

Theresa, this is my book. This is my tribute to you, and my gift to Madison, your beautiful child.

THOUGHTS FROM THE AUTHOR

When we are in the midst of happy times, contentment is so easily found from within and from those around us.

Conversely, when we are faced with difficulty, disappointment, and despair, we must be there for one another. It is a part of what gets us through many of life's "great tests," if you will.

Mothers, fathers, children, spouses, siblings, friends—we should not allow ourselves to foster or to contribute negatively to damaged or broken relationships. We never know when the ring of a telephone will impact our lives forever, in whatever manner.

When we die, we cannot take anything with us. But we can leave something behind. We can be remembered for being loving, caring, compassionate, forgiving, and for never being too proud to reach out to another when they need us. It can mean swallowing one's pride and expressing the importance of another human being in our lives to that person.

I am blessed with having been the recipient of great love from my child, my family, and my friends. I like to think that our relationships are something that we help to cultivate in each other.

God is Love. Love is Power. Without the two, life can be very sad and seem hopeless. But with them, no matter how long or how brief, life can be filled with happiness, contentment, and treasured memories.

We must all trust in God and follow His Word. He will lead us through the path of life with His Love.

CHAPTER ONE

It was Holy Week in April of 1962. On that Friday, Good Friday, she came to us.

As I looked at her beautiful, pink, perfectly shaped angelic face, I thought what a precious gift she is and she's as delicate as a "rosebud" in her pink bunting and fluffy yellow blanket. We would name her Theresa.

Our first miracle, Michael, who was a little more than three and one-half years older than she, was extremely excited about his new baby sister.

Tom had been so proud of his very special son and now of his wonderful little girl and I, Nancy, the mom just had it all!

We had the fulfillment of the "American Dream." We had a very happy marriage, a lovely home, and our two precious children to make the dream complete.

Over the years, as the children grew up, we kept involved with all the activities that are a part of raising a family. As all young couples do, we had our hills and valleys. There were times when

Tom was out of work due to company cutbacks. I was a stay-at-home mom, which was really important to both of us. This being the case, the entire responsibility of our family was on our protector, Daddy. He always provided well for us and was such a devoted family man.

It had been our fondest wish to be able to raise Michael and Theresa in a country atmosphere. We would always keep our eyes opened and our ears tuned in search of a country home.

I was glancing through the newspaper one Sunday in the spring of 1965. I came across an ad that read, "Ranch Style Home on 16 Acres." I got so excited. After I told Tom about it, he was as eager as I was to go see the property. He told me make an appointment. Luckily, we got one for that day.

With great anticipation, we all got into the car to go see it. We hoped so much that it would be what we had been looking for, as even back then, there weren't many homes available in our area with large parcels of land. At that time we owned an eight-year-old home in a relatively small development. The house was charming but we weren't really satisfied with the location. We just wanted a home in the country.

The Realtor was to meet us at the site. When we arrived, we drove into the very long driveway. It was like leaving one world and going into another--a wonderful one!

Before going into the house, which we could see was in need of considerable work, we walked the land. We looked at each other. We were sold! The field was beautiful. The trees were stately. There was one, in particular, a beautiful weeping willow, whose limbs seemed to embrace the shallow spring-fed pond, which nurtured it. The pond, teeming with turtles and frogs, would become Michael's source of nature's wonders and his own private waterway for his rowboat.

Theresa wasn't much into boats, turtles or frogs. Being the dainty little girl that she was, she loved sitting on a blanket with her doll babies, having a picnic, chasing butterflies and just being a pretty little "rosebud."

Our newfound home was a wonderful place, almost magical. It was perfect for children, pets and ponies and afforded great privacy.

There was a large barn on our little farm. So, of course, we needed animals. Michael loved his farm animals. We bought him a Black Angus calf named Doll. She was a real character. She used to sit with her front legs straight up and down and she would place her hindquarters on the ground, sitting up just like a dog. Michael had Doll for thirteen years. He had chickens, goats, rabbits, ducks and ponies. One pony was named Sugar; he was the gentle one. The other's name was Rusty; he was high spirited.

Michael took excellent care of his animals. Having them taught him responsibility. His dad taught him well. It was a wonderful way for a father and son to spend their time together.

The "rosebud"--well, she liked kittens, puppies, guinea pigs, and just about anything she could cuddle.

Buying our property was one of the best things we ever did for our children. When you come right down to it, it was the best thing for Tom and me, too. I loved being outdoors. I enjoyed working in the yard on my flowers and I got pleasure working in my vegetable garden. We used to start our own plants in the house in the early spring. Eventually, Tom started putting up a temporary greenhouse each year for me. We would start tomatoes, peppers, lettuce, eggplant and a large variety of flowers from seed. It was a good family activity. It was something we all enjoyed.

As time went on, we began to have work done on our home. All of the major things needed updating. Basically, we just about had the house rebuilt. It has been a very attractive and comfortable home for us over the years.

Tom decided it was time to buy some farm equipment. He felt it was important for our small farm to be self-sufficient. He purchased a tractor with all the necessary attachments, and kept Michael involved in the learning process of their new venture. He taught Michael a great deal about growing the hay for the animals, and getting the barn filled with hay for the winters. Being a highly principled man and a lover of nature, he is a firm believer that what you take from the land you must give back. He always stressed the importance of putting lime and fertilizer on the hayfields. He respects the land. Michael does too. To this day, they both love "haying season."

Some of the time, Tom worked the night shift. On summer afternoons, after he left for work, I'd pack a lunch for the beach and off the kids and I would go. We'd always have a great time. By the time we were arriving there most of the other kids and their moms were leaving. It was like having a private beach. The children would build sand castles, run, splash, tease each other and wear me out. Believe me, I loved every minute of it. Oh, the treasures we collect without even realizing it. Memories hover in the depths of our beings for us to draw on. They are so precious, just as priceless gems. As you read this, stop, think, and seize your special moments. Someday, they will be beautiful reflections of your past.

CHAPTER TWO

As time went by the kids got on with their schooling. Michael liked school and loved sports. He became involved with baseball, hockey and football. He was an outstanding hockey player.

Theresa wasn't very interested in sports. She preferred to make school her focus. She knew very early on that she wanted to be a teacher.

We continued to make improvements to our home. In 1976 Michael graduated from high school and Theresa graduated from middle school. We had an in-ground pool installed to celebrate the occasions. Michael was an avid swimmer and Theresa a sun worshiper.

The two had a very typical brother-sister relationship. At times, it seemed they could barely tolerate each other. However, one thing was for sure. They had a very strong, loving bond. They could always count on each other for the greatest support, no matter what situation they might find themselves in.

In the summers of 1978 and 1979 Theresa had worked as a volunteer teacher's aide with pre-school children who had Down's syndrome. She found the experience very rewarding. She loved the children. One day she and the teacher brought all of them to our home to see the farm animals. The little ones delighted in the whole outing. They ran and played outdoors and afterwards they all came in to have milk and cookies. As much fun as it was for the children, I think Theresa received the most pleasure of all. She beamed when she was with them. They appeared to be very attached to her. She loved the affection she received from them. Working with these very special children reinforced her determination to pursue a teaching career. That desire typified who she was. She was always so giving, whether to a friend, a child, family or to people on the whole.

She had many achievements in high school. She had served as class vice president, served on the student council, and was a member of the National Honor Society. In her yearbook her favorite saying was "if you love something, let it go; if it comes back it's yours; if it doesn't it never was." I often think of that saying these days.

Nineteen seventy-nine was a very big year for Michael. He married a wonderful girl, Patty, who became as a daughter to us. They had a marvelous wedding. It was a very emotional but happy day for Tom and me. It seemed as if Michael had reached manhood overnight. His departure from our home would be a tremendous adjustment for us. However, it was now time for him and Patty to start building on their hopes and dreams.

Nineteen eighty was a great year for Theresa. In June she graduated from high school. She was accepted to four colleges in the Boston area. Having made her choice, she would enter Northeastern University in Boston. She would major in Special Education.

We went on many a shopping spree. We bought clothes, personal items and all we could think of which she might need at school.

Finally, that momentous Sunday in late August arrived. It was time for her to embark on her college experience. We had spent most of that Saturday preparing for the next morning. Everything seemed to be in order. The station wagon was packed to bulging, and off the five of us headed for Northeastern University. We stopped on the way for breakfast, all having mixed emotions. We were happy for Theresa, but sad for us.

When we arrived on campus we had to unload the car and put her belongings on the sidewalk. Michael, Patty and Theresa were bringing her things into her dorm while Tom and I stayed there waiting for them to finish. Some of the upperclassmen helped in this effort, as was the tradition at Northeastern.

Standing next to Tom and me was a gentleman from Delaware whose daughter was also entering the university. He had everything from hotpot to hairdryer. We chatted briefly little realizing that his daughter Sandy and Theresa, for all subsequent years, would be the dearest of friends.

All of Theresa's things were now in the dorm. She would be sharing her room with one girl. Enter Nina! Here was this bouncy, free-spirited teenager who just HAD TO DO her hair with a curling iron before she could have her photo ID done.

I thought, what a meticulous girl. She's so fussy about her appearance. She must be a neatnik. WRONG! There will be more about Nina later!

How I dreaded saying good-bye to Theresa that day. Try as I might, I could not avoid a tearful farewell. We all shed some tears and told each other, "O.K. everything is all right, so let's head for home."

Tom, Patty, and I managed some degree of composure during the ride home. Michael, on the other hand, was still crying when we reached home one hour and forty miles later. Who would have believed that the little sister who could drive him to distraction during their childhood years could now bring him to tears? God love Michael.

In the weeks to come we would visit her at school weighted down with chocolate chip cookies, peanut butter cookies, raspberry squares, whoopie pies and many other goodies. I sure did cook a lot in those days. It seemed like the whole dorm used to wait for us to arrive.

We would walk into the room and it looked as if the two girls were living in different countries. Nina was soooo Nina, not very well organized. Theresa's side of the room had some semblance of order. Let me say, however, that what Nina lacked in orderliness, she made up for with her special warmth and charm.

They became such good friends and Nina, as Sandy, would forevermore, be a tremendously important part of Theresa's life.

Nina was from Connecticut. She and Theresa did so many things together. They had a great time exploring Boston and were truly enjoying the adventure of it all.

At one time they did some double dating. Nina's boyfriend, George, was her childhood sweetheart. Occasionally, when he would come to Boston to see her, he would bring a friend along. At one point he brought one of his lifelong friends, Gerald.

Theresa and Gerald dated a few times but both had former ties and nothing developed. She formed some great relationships in college. However, none of them seemed to have that special spark. That was all right. She was still young. Maybe someday it would happen.

CHAPTER THREE

As time went on, Theresa proved to be a very good student. She was on the Dean's List several semesters. How proud we were of her accomplishments.

As some readers may know, Northeastern has a cooperative education plan, which is a five-year program. After her freshman year, semester activities would alternate. One semester would consist of courses. During the next semester a student would work at a cooperative job placement. The work assignment would be focused on the student's major.

As Theresa's major was in Education, her co-op assignments were readily found in the greater Boston area.

Some of her experience was with pre-school children, whom she loved dearly. She and those children were featured in an article on the front page of the Boston Globe. There was a picture of the children and teachers from Park Street Children's Center playing ring-around-the-rosie at

Frog Pond in the Boston Common. Other assignments were with elementary school students. She always learned a great deal from these placements and gave back in equal measure. She found she enjoyed students of all ages.

One of her assignments, at Umana High School, was particularly challenging for Theresa. There was one Special Needs student who put her on notice her first day on the job that he had no intention of attending the Remedial Reading Class that she would be conducting. He meant what he had said. He didn't show up for class. She knew he was at school, so she made it her business to find him, collect him and march him promptly into class. For a few weeks he still showed much resistance and played his little games but I guess Theresa was the better player because at the end of her stay at that school he had become her biggest fan. Not only did she pride herself for this achievement, but she was also proud of that student. He demonstrated so much more maturity and self-confidence than he had when she began working with him. She felt gratified and she had also increased the faith that she had in her own abilities.

There was one semester coming when Theresa and Sandy decided that it would be sensational to do a co-op in Hawaii. Of course, when she ran this idea by her dad and me we saw it as totally unrealistic, absolutely impossible, and told her it did not merit further discussion.

I guess you just had to know Theresa. She had a fierce determination and a very winning way. Not only did we concede that it would be a good experience for the girls, but while in Hawaii in February of 1983, Tom and I rented a very pleasant efficiency apartment for them. It was high rise and it was secure. Most importantly, we knew first hand where they would be living. The girls were very excited about their trip. They left in the middle of March and returned to Boston at the end of May.

For about the first two weeks there, they were homesick but lo and behold they got over it and adjusted quite well.

They both got jobs with a telemarketing company. They did well on their jobs and were, for the most part, self-sufficient while they were there since they didn't have to pay rent. We talked to her twice a week.

Just imagine it, Tom and I waited for twenty-nine years to make it to Hawaii, and here was Theresa twenty-one years old staying for two months in Honolulu. I guess you could say we indulged her. Are we happy we did? You bet!

Through the rest of her college years she continued to excel academically. She maintained her close friendships with Nina and Sandy. Sometimes they would come home with her and spend the weekend with us. They were such good company, a true pleasure to be with.

CHAPTER FOUR

Finally in 1985, at the age of twenty-three, "the rosebud" graduated from college. We were so proud of her. Her graduation took place at the old Boston Garden in Boston's West End. After the ceremony her dad presented her with a dozen red roses. We returned home and had a marvelous party with many good friends and relatives there to shower congratulations upon her.

She moved back home and stayed with us for several months. We were happy to have her home again. We had been living the "empty nest syndrome" for too long.

At that time, teaching positions were not very plentiful and paid very little. Theresa did some substitute teaching in our hometown. She did enjoy it. The school year had come to an end. She wanted to find full-time employment.

Then the wanderlust struck again. She approached us with the idea that she might apply to a few airlines for a flight attendant position. We weren't thrilled with the prospect of all the flying this work would involve but she was enthusiastic. She sent out resumes and received an application from Eastern Airlines. She filled it out and sent it back. Within a few weeks she received a letter that, in essence, said that she must successfully complete the schooling and training program that was a prerequisite to being officially hired. She made arrangements to participate in the program. Now she would be preparing to go away again.

As I recall, it would require that she go to Florida for six weeks. We talked to her just about every day. She was homesick after being there for a couple of weeks but she was also busy and tired at day's end.

Being a flight attendant carries with it a great responsibility, the emphasis being on safety. The training was much more rigorous and physically demanding than she or we had imagined. She gave it her all and she succeeded. She was now officially a flight attendant for Eastern Airlines.

She called and said that she would be getting into Logan from Florida and wanted us to pick her up. We waited for her and when we saw her coming toward us she was in uniform and looked stunning, just beautiful. We stopped at a restaurant on the way home and took her to dinner. She had so much to tell us. We had missed her.

Within a few days she started work. She loved her job with the airline. Being a people-oriented person, she found it very interesting. She got to meet some celebrities. Once she was established on her job, she decided it would be a good idea for her to move closer to Boston. She and another of her friends, Danielle, rented an apartment in Swampscott together. It was in a great residential neighborhood and about twenty-five minutes from Logan.

Theresa garnered as much as she could from home for the new apartment. We also had a good time buying things for it. We helped the girls as much as we could, as did Danielle's parents. Between the two of them they ended up with a really attractive place to call home. She was close to the ocean and when she had time off she just loved spending her days at the beach. The seashore was always one of her favorite places, even as a child.

The household being in good order, Theresa started looking for a new car. She bought herself the Saab 900 she had been wanting and was even excited about having her very own thirty-six car payments, one of the fruits of adulthood. She was happy. All was right with the world.

All was right with Michael and Patty too. On April 3, 1986, they became the proud parents of Joshua Michael. We were thrilled to be grandparents and Theresa was at last an aunt.

Joshua's arrival was such a happy time for all of us. He was a darling baby. We all adored him.

Theresa was so pleased when Michael and Patty asked her to be Joshua's godmother. Patty's brother would be his godfather. He was baptized that June. We had a wonderful gathering at our home after the ceremony. It was a very joyous occasion. It's hard to believe that he is now eleven. He's a terrific boy and is an excellent student. He loves basketball; skateboarding, golf and "haying season" just like his dad and his grampa. Michael and Patty are very proud of him. We are, too.

CHAPTER FIVE

During that summer, as Theresa became more settled with her job and apartment, we managed to get together quite often for lunch and shopping. She had an insatiable appetite for shopping for both clothes and household items. Not surprisingly, she became quite proficient at it. She used to love to take me to the quaint shops in Marblehead. Most of the time we would have lunch at a place that overlooked the water. I always looked forward to our walk along the sea wall in Swampscott. Those were good times.

Not only had we been very close as mother and daughter over the years, but our relationship had also blossomed into a beautiful friendship. We were best friends and that feeling was a mutual thing. We both knew this because we told each other often. I'm so glad we were always able to speak of what was in our hearts. It's a very important part of everyone's life to be able to do that.

Theresa made several new friends at Eastern Airlines. The most special one was Colleen. She is just a wonderful girl and, I might add, also a marathon shopper. It's no small wonder that they gravitated to each other.

They used to fly together a lot and spend many of their days off with each other. Over the years they continued a very deep friendship. Like Theresa, Colleen was fun loving, warm and loved home and family. She is tremendously devoted to her parents, both very special people.

Colleen is still a flight attendant for a major airline. She has become a very important part of our lives. We thoroughly enjoy being with her. We love her dearly.

In October of 1986 Theresa thought it would be a great thing for her dad and me to take a trip with her to one of the Caribbean islands. We decided to go to St. Thomas. She got first class accommodations for all of us. We had a smooth flight. We first landed in Puerto Rico and then flew over to St. Thomas in a smaller, eighteen-passenger plane. I had been quite nervous at the prospect of flying in the small plane but it flew at a low altitude. Actually the flight was quite enjoyable. The ocean view, displaying such lovely hues of blue and green, was breathtaking. The seashore was so inviting. She and I were in our glory. Tom isn't much for the beach but Theresa and I couldn't get enough of it. He treated us like his queen and princess. We shopped 'til we dropped. Every meal was a sumptuous experience and the atmosphere was heavenly. Each evening we would have dinner at a castle in the hills. We dined out-of-doors. The breezes would billow through the branches of the tropical trees and the music from the piano bar was a special added touch.

It was a pleasant change for all of us and the memories are priceless. We had a marvelous time. I'm so happy we did that with her.

While still working for Eastern Airlines in 1987, the girls began to hear rumblings that the airline was in trouble and might have severe cutbacks or could shut down. Ultimately, that is what happened some time later. It is now defunct.

In June of 1987 Theresa heard about a job opening at the student placement office at Northeastern University. The position was for a career counselor.

Even though she enjoyed her job with the airline, she felt that it would be a good career move for her to apply at Northeastern University. Therefore she did.

She had her first interview and received mixed signals as to the possibility of her being hired. She was told that there were still ten more people to be interviewed.

She sent a thank you letter for the interview and again expressed her interest in the position.

She wanted the job so badly. Finally, they called her in for a second interview and to her great delight she was hired. This counseling position was her cup of tea. Things couldn't have been better. She was at her Alma Mater and she found it very rewarding working with the students. The challenge of coordinating the right cooperative job assignment for a particular student was most satisfying to her. However, in not one instance did she ever send one of them to Hawaii for a co-op assignment. How surprising! I wonder if it would have seemed unreasonable to her.

Here again she made some very good friends. There were Paula, Jeannie, Bill, Bob and Doc. Doc was her immediate supervisor. They got along very well and had a great deal of mutual respect. For all the years to come Theresa and Doc would keep in touch with each other.

While Theresa worked at Northeastern, Nina was working for a home health care company. She had majored in Respiratory Therapy. She traveled all over New England on her job.

Sandy had moved back to Delaware. I believe she was in sales. She would later marry her college sweetheart, Mark. Theresa had the pleasure of being a bridesmaid in their wedding.

Colleen was still flying. From time to time Theresa still managed to get together with each of her friends.

Quite frequently, Patty and I would meet her in the city. We would go to dinner and the theater. We all loved musicals. Looking back, I wish we had done more of that. Theresa used to like to take us to the Top of the Hub, Fanueil Hall Market place and to many of Boston's fine restaurants. When she was in school she used to like her dad and me to take her to Friday's for dinner. It's a fun place to go. Another of her favorites was Legal Seafood. She absolutely loved seafood. She especially enjoyed my homemade fish chowder and lobster pie. One or the other was always a must whenever she came home.

She loved the city and all it had to offer from theater, to the Boston Pops, museums, historical sites, fine cuisine, sporting events and the stores. In particular, she enjoyed going to the shops on Newbury Street. I'm so pleased that she had the opportunity to enjoy so much of what Boston has to offer.

CHAPTER SIX

I can remember Theresa asking me over the years, "Mom, how do you know when you're in love?" I would answer, "You just know." She was beginning to think it wouldn't happen for her. She dated quite a bit but by no means was she a social butterfly.

Sometimes we would talk and anticipate about if, and when, she would marry. She would say, "Please don't you and dad ever move until I get married. I want to be married from my home." That meant a great deal to her.

In April of 1988 Nina became engaged. Remember George, her childhood sweetheart? Well, he definitely was "the one" for Nina. Theresa was so happy for her. On Veteran's Day weekend, on November 11, 1988, Nina and George were married in Connecticut. Of course, Theresa went to the wedding. She was asked to do a reading from scripture during the Mass. She was honored.

She didn't bring a guest. She was kind of hoping that she might run into "that fellow" Gerald, whom she had dated a few times during her freshman year at Northeastern University. Do you recall? He was George's friend. As fate would have it, Gerald didn't bring a guest either. He was kind of hoping he might run into "that girl" Theresa, whom he had dated a few times during her freshman year at Northeastern University. Well, after eight years, they met again. They had a good time getting reacquainted and just enjoyed each other's company immensely. That would be the beginning of the happiest years of Theresa's life.

She came home from the wedding on Monday. She was aglow. She couldn't wait to fill me in on Gerald. Maybe she didn't know that day that he was "the one" but I certainly did.

A mother waits her daughter's lifetime to see that special twinkle in her eye, that special smile that a mention of his name can bring to her. Theresa had that twinkle and smile.

They continued to see each other over the next several months. Theresa was happier than I had ever seen her.

When she introduced us to Gerald, what I noticed about him, immediately, were his smiling eyes. If his heart was as kind as his eyes, I knew Theresa had found herself a man very much like her dad. What more could I have wanted for her?

The following summer we went to Connecticut to meet Gerald's family. They were wonderful and it was quite apparent that they were as taken with Theresa as we were with Gerald.

We were having a barbecue at our home one beautiful June day. Gerald took Tom and me aside to tell us that within a couple of weeks he intended to propose to Theresa and would like our blessing and approval. We told him that, "We couldn't be happier."

In July 1989 they became engaged. Gerald gave her an absolutely gorgeous diamond. She was overjoyed. They were so happy. Both families were delighted.

Soon after their engagement, they set the date for the wedding. It would be on February 17, 1990. Being a golf pro, spring, summer and fall were so busy for him at the golf course they decided that a winter wedding would be most practical.

The date being set, Theresa decided to give up her apartment with Danielle and move back home to save some money.

This had to be one of the most exciting times of our lives. Tom was a wreck wondering what kind of wedding plans we would come up with and I couldn't wait to get started. Theresa gave me great latitude but she had the very final word on things.

How exciting it would be to arrange for Saint Joseph's Church, which is a magnificent edifice, the organist, the vocalist and what a thrill it would be shopping for her wedding gown. We had gone on many excursions looking for her gown but in the end Theresa chose the very first gown she had tried on weeks before. It was of elegant white satin with hand-sewn pearls and lace and it had a cathedral-length train. It was an exquisite creation.

I vividly remember the day she picked out her veil. After selecting it, she tried on both her gown and headpiece. She was up on the platform with the consultant making sure everything was perfect. Indeed it was. She was a vision of beauty far beyond description. At least in a mother's eyes she was. This mother's eyes welled up with tears that were the product of a wide array of emotions.

Theresa, Patty and I went shopping for my dress. That was a pleasure. I had chosen my dress early on and had also bought some of my accessories. Everything met with Theresa's approval. She graciously bought my jewelry. It was lovely. I will always treasure it. She had excellent taste.

Patty would be the matron of honor. The bridesmaids were Nina, Theresa's cousin Cindy, who was more like a sibling to her, and Gale and Gwen, Gerald's two sisters.

Now what color would the bridesmaids wear? The decision being made, it would be a black and white wedding. The girls would wear black velvet gowns, which I designed. We had looked at so many gowns but none seemed to be what Theresa and the girls were looking for. After I came up with a style that they all approved of, we engaged a local dressmaker to make them.

The groom, groomsmen and ring bearers would wear black tuxes. Joshua and Gerald's nephew Michael would be ring bearers.

Things were really getting very well organized. The invitations were ordered, the limousines and the photographer booked, the cake selected, the Andover Country Club was reserved for the reception, the band was booked and the flowers were chosen. Although Theresa's favorite flowers were tulips, they were not conducive to being used in a bouquet. The bridal bouquet would be made of red and white roses. She loved roses. The bridesmaids would carry red and white roses, carnations, and stephanotis. What a beautiful combination the flowers would be with the black velvet gowns.

All of the preparations had gone so smoothly. Theresa told me that I should start a business as a wedding consultant and planner. I had enjoyed all of the preliminaries so much.

Patty and Cindy planned a bridal shower for Theresa. They had it at Saint Joseph Parish Hall on a Sunday. There was a terrible blizzard that day but nevertheless almost every invited guest showed up. It certainly was an affirmation of their love for Theresa. The girls had done a great job. The shower was a huge success.

Just prior to the wedding, Gerald brought the tuxes from Connecticut. When Tom tried his on, he called me into the bedroom. We started laughing hysterically. The kids thought we had taken leave of our senses. That is until we came out to show them what we were laughing about and then they joined in the laughter. There was Tom, almost 5'11", in his tux that fit great except that the trousers had an inseam of 24 inches. His inseam is 29 inches. Picture it! It was hilarious. It still makes me smile when I think about it. I can still picture those five extra inches of ankles and legs showing.

The night of the rehearsal dinner was a very special night for the kids but it was also very special for me. It was my birthday. The dinner had gone very well. Gerald's mom had reserved the upstairs room of a very popular restaurant in Newburyport. The ambiance was delightful and the food was impeccable.

Theresa, Tom, and I got home that night around 11:45 p.m. Tom kissed us goodnight and went to bed. Theresa and I stayed up and talked. She said, "Mom I want you to have this tonight." It was a beautiful poem about "Mother." I read it and of course I cried. I was so moved by it and felt so blessed to have this very special young woman for my daughter. We hugged and spoke of our great love for each other.

I have the poem displayed on the wall. I read it quite often and sometimes it still makes me cry.

CHAPTER SEVEN

The big day had come! It was brisk and brilliant. The sun couldn't have been brighter.

Not long after we were up, the house was abuzz with excitement. The florist came. The girls came to get dressed. Tom and I got ready and with Patty's help Theresa finished getting dressed. She came out of her room. She was an absolute vision.

The photographer arrived and took many pictures. All of the girls looked lovely and were bubbling with excitement. The pictures being done, we were ready to leave for the church. The girls gathered their bouquets and got into the first limo.

Tom then helped his precious "little girl" into the other limo. How mixed his emotions must have been but he loved her enough to let her go. He was confident that she was going to a wonderful young man. A father can take great comfort in that thought when he truly believes it and I know Tom did. It was a glorious day, a day of great beginning.

Some 185 guests were waiting at the church. They had come from Pennsylvania, New York, Delaware, New Hampshire, Connecticut and from many parts of Massachusetts.

Our son Michael, one of Gerald's groomsmen, walked his grandmother, my mother, down the aisle. How very lucky we were to have her there at age 78 and still an energetic, pretty lady.

After my mom was seated, Michael came back to escort me to my seat. Gerald's brother George, also a groomsman, escorted his mother, Mary, down the aisle. I know that both of our hearts were filled with joy to be present at the union of our two marvelous children. The vocalist sang Ave Maria as Mary and I advanced to our places. It was very moving. Mary and I then went up to the altar to light the Unity Candle that symbolized Theresa and Gerald's commitment to each other and the joining of our families. I feel it was a true expression of what was in all our hearts.

Everyone in place, it was time for Theresa to come and meet her groom. The bridesmaids looked beautiful as they walked forward and the ring bearers were so precious.

The organist played the exuberant processional and I saw Theresa and her dad coming. She was absolutely breathtaking. She was smiling but her eyes were also filled with tears. I was so proud of her and so filled with hope for her future.

There was her Gerald waiting for her with such great love in his "smiling eyes." What a gift he was for our dear daughter. Her dad kissed her on the cheek, ever so gently, and presented this beautiful treasure to her love.

Their wedding was celebrated with a Nuptial Mass. Sandy read a passage from scripture, and Theresa's special childhood friend, Diane, read another. The priest spoke a Papal Blessing over them and joined them in Holy Matrimony. At the conclusion of the Mass, they were presented to their families and friends as Mr. and Mrs., and they were both beaming as they descended from the altar. The church was resounding with the melodious strains of the recessional hymn and applause from all those who had witnessed this momentous time in the lives of these two special people.

We then had the receiving line at the church where each guest could share their moment with the bride and groom and their families. Afterward, we went on to the country club where there would be many more pictures taken.

A great selection of hors-d'ouvres awaited the guests. Music filled the air. The room, with fireplace, was enchanting. The meal was beautifully presented and I believe enjoyed by all. It was such a joyous occasion but also a very emotional time. I still feel a fleeting moment of sadness when I hear the song "Daddy's Little Girl" as I reach back into my memory and picture Theresa's dance with her dad. Oh, how he loved her and how we would miss having her with us.

Both families gathered at our home after the reception. We were still riding the waves of excitement from the fantastic celebration.

Theresa and Gerald were picked up by limousine and headed to the airport. They left for a two-week honeymoon trip. They went to Honolulu, Mauai and then to San Diego.

When they returned, Theresa picked up her roots from Massachusetts and planted them very firmly in Connecticut, with Gerald, the love of her life.

CHAPTER EIGHT

Although it was a big transition for Theresa, Gerald and his family made it an easy one for her. They are a close family and they welcomed her with open arms. We didn't worry about her because we knew she was surrounded with people who loved her. She responded to them in kind.

Not only was his family warm and welcoming, so were Gerald's friends. There is a closely-knit group of young couples who seem to stick together through thick and thin. I have developed a special affection for many of them.

Theresa and Gerald had a lovely condo. It was in a pleasant country location. They would often see deer grazing in the field beyond their yard. The condo was beautifully decorated. They both liked nice things and had good taste. Theresa loved being a homemaker. They were enjoying married life. They were truly committed to each other.

Eventually, she found a job with Estee Lauder at one of the large department stores. She made more special friends. She was a great representative for the company as she had extreme beauty, both inner and outer, and she had personality plus. Eventually, she achieved manager's status. She did well.

She became very attached to one of her co-workers, Jane. She used to tell me how fortunate she felt to have met her. Jane helped to make Theresa's work pleasurable.

Theresa called me one day and was very concerned about Jane. She had been diagnosed with cancer. Theresa was so worried about her and was greatly relieved when after treatment Jane got a clean bill of health.

After I met this very special friend of Theresa's, it was easy to understand why she was so fond of her. I still talk to Jane from time to time. I enjoy her. She is so warm and gracious.

The months went by and the newlyweds were happy and doing well. Gerald was very busy at the golf course and occasionally Theresa would come home for a short visit by herself.

One delightful September day in 1991, I came home after doing errands. I found Theresa asleep on the sofa. It was a welcome surprise to have her come up from Connecticut. We gave each other a kiss and I asked her if she felt all right. She smiled and said, "I was just having a little nap." She said she had been feeling tired lately and smiled again, only this time more broadly. Yes, she was pregnant!

I was on Cloud Nine and so was she. When her dad came in she told him and we were ecstatic. Patty and Joshua stopped for a visit and Theresa shared the tremendous news with her. I couldn't believe this great blessing. Once again, we would be grandparents and our dear "rosebud" would be a mom. As one would expect, Gerald was bursting with joy when we called to congratulate him. Now he would have another treasure to add to his life.

A few weeks went by. They were going for Theresa's ultrasound. She asked us if we wanted to know if it would be a boy or a girl. We told her "No," we wanted to be surprised. She agreed that she wouldn't tell us.

The ultrasound went fine and she asked again if we wanted to know because she and Gerald knew; again we said "No."

The weeks went by and her pregnancy seemed to be going well. She was radiant and just beautiful. Then one day we were talking about "the baby." Theresa slipped and said, "She's really getting very active." She just couldn't stand for us not to know. Of course we were thrilled. We would now have our Joshua and our new granddaughter. How blessed we were.

Theresa asked me if I would make some maternity outfits for her. I made several. She loved them and I loved doing it.

For the baby I knitted and crocheted sweaters, booties and a carriage robe. Also, I sewed two comforters and complete sets of matching bumper pads for the crib. My next project was making curtains for the nursery.

Theresa had put a great deal of thought into decorating it. She used a very feminine theme, flowers and ribbons, just perfect for a baby girl. They bought an unfinished armoire and had it decorated by a very talented woman who painted it white and then painted flowers and ribbons on it. She also applied the same decor to a rocking chair, a mirror, and a dresser. The pieces were so dainty looking. The baby would have a very inviting room. Everything had come together quite beautifully.

We had countless discussions about what they would name her. Would it be Alexandra, Angela, Christina, Sarah, or so many other choices? No, it would be Madison--Madison Marie to be exact.

That April we had a baby shower for her. This one was also at the parish hall as her bridal shower had been. Gerald's sister had another one in Connecticut for her. The baby would want for nothing. Her daddy had bought her coming-home outfit for her. It was one of the gifts at the shower Gale gave Theresa. It was an adorable white outfit with pink satin rosebuds on it. He was so anxious for her arrival. Everything was ready and waiting for her.

At about 7:00 a.m. on May 18, 1992 we got a call from Gerald. He called to let us know that Theresa was in the hospital in labor. I had packed our bags weeks before so we left not long after getting his call. The two of us were a wreck. We had prayed so hard for all those months that the delivery would be an easy one and that the baby would be healthy.

When we arrived in Connecticut we went to the condo and waited to hear from Gerald. He kept us posted periodically. Finally, at around 2:00 p.m. he called again to tell us that Madison was born and that she and Theresa were doing fine. He said, "Mom, I was so proud of Theresa, you should have seen how great she did." Theresa would tell us later that he did "fantastic" himself.

We went to the hospital later that evening to see them. Theresa and Gerald were so happy. Gerald, beaming with pride, brought us to the nursery to see the baby. She, of course, was beautiful and very vocal. It was as if she were announcing, "O.K. world, here I am." We were all overjoyed, relieved, and so grateful.

We didn't stay at the hospital too late. We wanted Theresa to get some rest. It had been a long day for Gerald, too. The next day we went in to see them and we got to hold our granddaughter for the first time. What a thrill it was. The new parents were as pleased for us as we were for them.

I had the pleasure of spending a week with them when Theresa and the baby came home. I was definitely in my glory. How I loved my two girls.

After a week's time Tom came to get me. He was eager to see the baby and the new parents again. We stayed and visited for a while so that Tom could renew his acquaintance with his new "little girl." He would eventually become Pop Pop to Madison and I would become Nana.

Later that day we left for home. They were on their own.

CHAPTER NINE

Gerald, from day one, was an outstanding dad. Madison was a colicky baby. Therefore, none of them got much sleep for several months. He always shared in the care of his "Bella." That is what he affectionately called her.

They both absolutely adored their darling child. I can picture Theresa now looking at and talking to Madison. She would say, in a happy, stimulating voice, "How is my beautiful, darling baby girl?" Baby girl would get so excited. She would get her hands and feet moving and would squeal with excitement. How many times did she say that to her and how I would love to hear it again.

Madison was christened in July. Michael was her godfather and Gale was her godmother. The christening was a memorable celebration with family and friends.

Tom and I decided to make it a special family weekend. We stayed at a nearby Holiday Inn with Michael, Patty, and Joshua. Joshua had a grand time. He got to enjoy the indoor swimming pool and the exercise room. We ordered room service and he thought it was the greatest thing. Theresa came over to the hotel in the morning with Madison and joined us for breakfast. We stopped at her house on the way back. It had been a very good weekend.

Before we knew it a year had gone by. Madison had her first birthday. It was a wonderful party. She was already walking. She had started at nine months old when they were in Florida that February while visiting Mary, Madison's Memom. This little toddler was such a bundle of energy.

As they accumulated more things for Madison and she became increasingly active, they started thinking about selling their condo. They needed more space. The real estate market wasn't very good at the time but luckily they found a buyer.

They had been looking at property and having found nothing they wanted, they decided to have a home built. The house would be an eight-room Colonial style with two and one-half bathrooms, a two-car garage and was situated on three-quarters of an acre. It was just what they wanted. The yard would be perfect for Madison. Theresa had a wonderful time coordinating the decor. She did a very professional job. Everything looked great.

Happily, they moved into their new home in June 1994. Madison was two. Theresa was an "at-home mom." Gerald was doing well at work.

I guess you could say that they had achieved their "American Dream."

Theresa made an effort to come for a visit about once a month. Gerald had to work six days a week, so she would drive up with Madison and maybe stay for a couple of days. My mother always loved it when they came for those delightful visits.

She came home in early March. Gerald had started back to work. The weather was perfect while they were here. We took Madison to the park and spent many hours outdoors with her. She loved going down to the barn to see the horses and at that time we had a calf. She used to get so excited about the animals. The horses are named Mac and Tosh. She loved bringing apples and carrots to them. Sweetie, our cat, was most special to Madison. Theresa had brought her to me as a kitten on Mother's Day eight years earlier.

One of Theresa's favorite things to do when she came home was to go get some "beach pizza." She just had to have some pizza from Salisbury Beach. We always had to go and have our fill.

Things seemed great that night after having had two fun-filled days with them. Theresa was sitting on the sofa with Madison and was cuddling with her. Madison had already been bathed and was in her pajamas and looked as shiny and bright as a new penny. As I sat there and looked at them I thought, Theresa, what a charmed life you have had. My thoughts were that she had tremendous physical beauty, incomparable inner beauty, and now this wonderful family. Everything was perfect. The visit had been so enjoyable. The next day they went home.

I don't know why but the day after they left, I had been thinking of Theresa so much I just felt I must write to her and tell her just how very special she was to me. She called me after she received the letter and said, "Gee whiz, Mom, you made me cry." I told her I hadn't meant for her to cry but I just had to express my thoughts to her in writing.

A couple of weeks went by and we started looking forward to Theresa's birthday in April, when we would see them again.

CHAPTER TEN

It was the twenty-third of March 1995. It was around dinnertime. Theresa called me. She immediately started to cry. I couldn't imagine what was wrong. I tried to calm her down to find out what was upsetting her so. She said, "Mom, I have breast cancer." I think my heart stopped momentarily. This couldn't be happening! I struggled to stay composed and I asked her what the doctor had said. She told me she had to have a mastectomy. We were devastated.

This was unbelievable. She had had her annual checkup about a month or six weeks prior to this. She got a clean bill of health. Of course, she was only thirty-two so she had had no mammogram. Theresa discovered the lump herself while taking a shower. One can only imagine and speculate as to how long this cancer had been growing before it manifested itself.

How would I break this news to my mother? We let Michael and Patty know that evening but it took me two days to find the courage to tell her grandmother. Finally I did. She was heartbroken. I tried to give her all the reassurance I could but in my heart I was having a difficult time reassuring myself. Tom and I felt as if our world was falling apart. He, my rock, after a great deal of inner turmoil, said to me, "We have to be strong and positive for Theresa and Gerald. They need us." I wouldn't have expected less from Tom. He is so giving and is always able to show me the way. He said, "We have to face this thing head on," and so we would.

On April 10, we celebrated Theresa's birthday at their home in Connecticut. We were all on an emotional roller coaster. Our beautiful daughter would have a modified radical mastectomy on April 11, her thirty-third birthday.

When she was leaving the house that morning, I looked into her loving blue eyes and said, "Theresa, I have no words," she said, "I know Mom." I kissed her, her dad kissed her and she and Gerald left for the hospital in Hartford where Madison had been born. I cried, for my heart was broken.

She would later tell us that upon arriving at the hospital and being prepared for surgery they said that she could probably go home that night at eight-o'clock. Can you imagine? I found this extremely disturbing. In retrospect, I feel that this was a preview of what is now going on in the medical profession with inpatient care.

Madison would keep us busy that day. Tom kept himself occupied assembling a battery-powered Jeep that we had bought for her. She would be three in May and we thought she would love riding around her yard in it. She and I kept checking on Pop Pop's progress and we spent most of the day outdoors. She loved her yard and her swingset.

As the day went on, we were anxiously waiting to hear about Theresa. The waiting seemed to go on forever. By midafternoon Gerald called us from the hospital. Theresa's surgery had taken longer than we had expected. He said she had come through it fine and was doing all right. She ended up spending two days in the hospital and was released on the third day. In fact, I believe it was Good Friday.

Tom and I stayed until Easter Sunday. Late that morning we headed back to Massachusetts. We were all relieved that Theresa's surgery was behind her. Now they could get on with their lives.

Ten days after her operation, she went in for her follow-up examination. The doctor told her and Gerald that she had removed thirty-one lymph nodes during the surgery and twenty-three of them tested positive for cancer. This was not good news! The doctor classified her cancer as stage Two and described it as very aggressive. She told them that she strongly recommended that Theresa have a bone marrow transplant. It was her professional opinion that the transplant would be the best chance for no recurrence of the cancer. Theresa and Gerald were in shock, dumbfounded.

She called to tell us about her doctor's visit and again, she was in tears. My immediate thought was what if we can't find a match. Even the thought of it made me feel physically ill. What was happening? All of our lives were all in a tailspin especially Theresa and Gerald's.

I told Tom after I hung up the phone. We just felt numb. Our hearts were so very heavy at this distressing news.

Subsequently, they consulted with three other oncologists, all independent of each other. After evaluating Theresa's records each one recommended that she have a bone marrow transplant.

This just couldn't be. It didn't make sense. She was thirty-three. She was a young wife and mother. You know what people think. We think, "These things happen to other people." Then come one day, we can be those "other people."

Standard chemotherapy and radiation were also an option to her but all of the doctors favored the transplant procedure. This was such a difficult decision for her and Gerald to make.

One large concern had been addressed. If Theresa decided to have the transplant procedure, a donor would not be necessary. The protocol the doctors were suggesting would eliminate the search for a compatible donor. Through the process proposed, she would be her own donor.

CHAPTER ELEVEN

Theresa had tremendous faith. Prayer had become a constant companion to her. Her patron saint was Saint Theresa, "The Little Flower." In all depictions of her, whether it be a picture or a statue, she is always holding a cross and roses. There was a song in the 50's called "Saint Theresa of the Roses." I was a teenager then but I can remember being very partial to the song. I used to pray to Saint Theresa myself for the arrival of our children. Therefore, we named Theresa after her. It seemed appropriate to do so.

One morning during the course of her trying to make her decision on what treatment to have, she asked her patron saint for guidance because she was so confused.

Shortly after, she received a phone call from the University of Connecticut Health Center. They were calling to inform her that their facility had a bone marrow transplant protocol in place. I assume that her doctor had asked them to call Theresa.

She talked to the coordinator and told her she would be willing to come in and discuss the matter. The girl entered Theresa's name in the computer to set up the meeting. Much to her surprise Theresa's previous address came up, her date of birth and her Social Security Number. She asked Theresa if she had ever been a patient there. She said, "No." Furthermore, she had been at their new address for almost a year. The girl's next comment was "There's something very strange about this." Theresa asked why and the coordinator told her that the patient number that came up on the screen for her was, "Off the wall." It was unlike any patient number in their system. They were both puzzled as to how she was already in the computer and as to why her old address was showing up. Was this a sign?

I had been to church. I tried to go every morning. When I came home Tom said, "Call Theresa right away. She called and she was crying, it's something about Saint Theresa." I called and she told me about this unusual happening. She was very emotional.

As if they didn't have enough problems, there was also cause for further concern. Gerald had taken a new health insurance policy about a week before Theresa discovered the lump in her breast. Because the policy was so new, the insurance company was refusing to acknowledge payment responsibility for her treatment starting with the cost of the mastectomy and all other costs related to it. Theresa and Gerald could foresee a large problem with the cost of the bone marrow transplant if she underwent the procedure. They suspected the insurance company would resist paying for it. They would be proven right.

Theresa and Gerald kept the appointment at the University Health Center. It was for a family conference. At their request, I went with them. The doctor was very reassuring. He explained the whole procedure, in laymen's terms, quite thoroughly. It was a great deal to absorb and, moreso, an awful lot to accept.

We had all listened intently while the presentation was being made. At the conclusion, Theresa looked at the doctor and bravely asked, "When can we get started?" She said, "If I do this I'll know that I did all I could do to fight the cancer." She had so much to live for.

Theresa would be participating in a clinical trial since this treatment was still considered experimental for breast cancer patients. It had been in use for several years to treat patients with lymphoma. From what I understand, it was used with a good degree of success.

For the treatment of breast cancer it had a history of about two years in 1995 when Theresa agreed to participate. We were all hopeful that this would eliminate the return of her cancer.

The transplant procedure would be autologous. This procedure uses the stem cells from the patient's own blood. The stem cells are collected through a procedure called pheresis. They are analyzed, treated, and returned to the patient in about three months, after all the appropriate steps of the transplant procedure have taken place. In the interim the stem cells are kept frozen.

The fact that the insurance company was refusing to pay was extremely upsetting and so very wrong. I wrote a letter to the office of the insurance commissioner of Connecticut and sent with it all the documentation that we could provide. It was maddening wondering what would happen.

Madison's third birthday was just around the corner. Theresa was still recuperating from her April surgery and simultaneously preparing herself physically and mentally for the months to come.

Her immediate concern, however, was making sure that Madison would have a wonderful birthday party. Although her birthday was on May 18, they planned her party for May 21, which was a Saturday.

Diane and Mae, her mother, and I went to Connecticut for it. Diane had always been very faithful about visiting Theresa in Connecticut from the time she was married. The three of us used to go down about every other month. We always had a good time. Theresa loved those visits.

Theresa and Gerald had arranged for Barney, the Purple Dinosaur, and Snow White to be at the party. All the children were filled with excitement. They were adorable.

I marveled at Theresa's positive, unselfish attitude as I watched her that day. She was so upbeat for Madison. She played ring-around-the-rosie with the kids. That brought me back in time to the article about Theresa and the pre-schoolers at Frog Pond on the Boston Common that had been in the newspaper so many years before.

All of the birthday guests stayed. These were some of the dear friends she had been blessed with through her marriage. They were all very concerned about her and were ready to lend their support to all of us.

That day was a very emotional one for me. What I remember most was trying to keep from crying. I couldn't get my mind off what was ahead for Theresa. I was petrified but I always tried not to let Theresa and Gerald know it. I'm sure they hid those same fears from me. I couldn't begin to imagine how they must feel. My heart ached for them and there was nothing I could do to ease their pain.

CHAPTER TWELVE

On May 25, 1995 Theresa was admitted to the hospital for three days of chemotherapy, the first round. First they would implant a port catheter into her right chest. This would enable her to receive the chemo and any intravenous administrations through the catheter. This way they would also be able to draw blood, which would have to be done countless times over at least the next six months. The catheter would eliminate the use of needles for all the procedures to follow.

I was with Theresa when the nurse started the first infusion of chemo. All I could think about was that I couldn't bear to see these toxins going into our beautiful daughter. The world seemed so upside down.

Thank God, Gerald's sister Gale came in just after Theresa had started with the chemo. We sat and talked with her. Her friend Jane also stopped by the hospital to visit her. I think, subconsciously, we were all trying to distract each other from what was really taking place. Theresa was very courageous. She knew what a long road she had ahead of her over the next several months. Jane had to leave for work. Gale and I stayed awhile longer. When she appeared to be comfortable, Gale and I told her to get some rest and we left. When we were out of Theresa's sight I just clung to Gale and I cried. She was a great comfort to me. I will always remember her kindness. The reality of what was happening seemed more than I could endure.

Gerald, of course, had to work while Theresa was in the hospital but without fail, every night, he would first come home to check on Madison and spend some time with her. Then he would go to the hospital to see Theresa. He would stay with her until she was settled for the night.

On the fourth day she came home. She was very sick from the chemo. She was so sick she said to me, as I sat on the edge of her bed, "Mom, I don't think I want to do this." I had a feeling of helplessness. I said, "Theresa, you've started now. You can't turn back." She said, "I just hate this so much," and she cried. How I wanted to take this burden from her.

For the next two days she had a great deal of nausea and difficulty keeping anything in her stomach. She appeared bewildered. Gerald was so concerned and, oh, so good to her. He is really quite remarkable, a pillar of strength.

Gradually the vomiting subsided. We were all tremendously relieved when Theresa could start to take nourishment again.

I would now have a new challenge. I had to learn how to care for the catheter. The dressing needed to be changed every day. I was quite nervous about doing it. I had to wear a mask, as did Theresa. She knew it made me feel breathless, but for her I could do it. She said to me as I was changing the dressing the first time, "Mom, when this is all over, you and I are going to go on a talk show." We laughed about her comment. I think she was silently, lovingly, laughing at my eagerness to get that mask off. She could always read me so well.

Theresa had beautiful long hair when she was diagnosed. Prior to starting the chemotherapy treatment she got a short hair cut. She looked like a doll. She knew that her hair would fall out within about two weeks after her first round of chemo. I think that was the most difficult emotional adjustment she had to make. As was so typical of her positive approach to things, she said one morning, "Let's go to the wig place today. I need to have my wig fitted." So off we went. While we were there she said to Owen, the fellow fitting the wig, "Please cut my hair as short as you can," and he did almost shave her head. Within the next few days all of her hair had fallen out. Even so, she was still beautiful.

In the event the insurance company would agree to pay her medical expenses, Theresa and Gerald would still be responsible for a great deal of the cost that would not be covered by insurance. Knowing this, Gerald's two sisters, Gale and Gwen, decided to organize a fund-raiser for them. They approached the Kelly family who owns the golf course where Gerald works about having a golf tournament to benefit Theresa.

They generously agreed to donate the course for the day of the fund-raiser that would be June 8, 1995. They were wonderful about it. They did all they could to help. They are very special people. Long before Theresa became ill, Gerald used to say that "The Kelly boys are like brothers to me," and indeed they are.

The response from the public was phenomenal. The tournament was a huge success. The girls and some family friends had also organized a raffle on several items donated, at their request, by many business people. They all gave so willingly. It was amazing.

After the golf tournament, all participants were invited back to a function hall for an appreciation luncheon. The use of the hall had been donated. Friends and relatives contributed and prepared great amounts of food. It was a wonderful day, Theresa's Day. Theresa and I weren't able to attend but we got a detailed report from Gerald and the family. All those who participated in this wonderful effort will never know how deeply it was appreciated by Theresa, Gerald, and by their families. The tournament and raffle had raised a great deal of money for them and were such a tremendous expression of love and moral support from so many warm and caring people.

It gave them great peace of mind in so far as the financial hurdles they would have to deal with.

She had a few weeks to recuperate from the first round of chemo. She started feeling quite well.

Within a matter of five or six weeks after Theresa's treatment had started, thank heavens, the University Health Center notified her that the insurance company had agreed to pay its share for the very costly treatment. We were tremendously relieved and thankful for this outcome. It was the first we had heard since my sending the letter to the insurance commission. Their intervention and support were sincerely appreciated.

Theresa was able to be home for the Fourth of July. We were invited to the home of Gerald's brother George for a barbecue that day. He and his wife, Lynn, had gone all out to make it special. George is a wonderful cook and a great guy. He is always recruited to oversee the menu and to do the food preparation whenever there's a family gathering. Everyone enjoyed the day.

We got home from their house and awaited the fireworks. Theresa, Gerald, Madison, and I watched them from their own backyard. She was happy to be home for the holiday. Madison loved the beautiful, bright display. She squealed with excitement for each one. She called them fire engines.

CHAPTER THIRTEEN

The next morning, July 5, Theresa was again admitted to the hospital for another three-day stay for the second round of chemotherapy. All of the staff members were wonderful to her. They were like old friends by now. On the fourth day she was released. Although she had experienced some bouts of nausea and vomiting while in the hospital, when she came home she seemed to tolerate the effects of the chemo better than she had the first time. I also think we were more aware of how to manage those side effects based on her coping with the first round. Within a few days of coming home she had found a fairly good comfort zone. She wouldn't have to be admitted to the hospital again until August, although we made numerous trips to the outpatient Bone Marrow Transplant Clinic for her blood studies. We used to go in every third or fourth day. It was important for them to keep a close eye on her blood counts.

From the time of her diagnosis, Nina, Sandy, Colleen, and many of her friends in Connecticut kept in close touch with Theresa. They were still such devoted friends. They were also very considerate of me in that they gave me great moral support through all of this and they still do.

When Theresa was going through her treatment, Diane organized a fund-raiser at our church. At Diane's request, the choir agreed to put on a bake sale at church one weekend in August. They also raffled off a beautiful food basket of Italian delicacies. Hundreds of tickets were sold.

I was a choir member, although I had not been in attendance since that previous April. They are an extremely caring group.

Their doing this for Theresa touched my heart more than I could ever say. The parishioners demonstrated wholehearted support for the fund-raiser. Diane called us in Connecticut late that Sunday to tell us that they had raised $2,200 for Theresa. It was unbelievable to us that such a large amount had been realized through this concerted effort. It told me that not only did Diane, the choir, and other generous people who contributed baked goods cared, but also how caring our Church community was. I know that so many of these good people prayed for Theresa as well as for Gerald, Madison, and our families. Prayer had been our mainstay.

Theresa's fifteen-year high school reunion was on Saturday, August 13. Obviously, she and

Gerald could not attend. Her friend Raylene had made two very large posters for her classmates to sign. We would be leaving early on Sunday the fourteenth for Connecticut. In the wee hours of the morning Raylene put the posters in our car and we took them to Theresa. It was a great surprise to her and so appreciated. Those who signed it wrote words of encouragement to Theresa and reflected many reminiscences of their younger days. Her lifelong friend Kimiko had stopped at our home before the reunion with a card and a note to Theresa. She was very emotional as we spoke about Theresa's illness and so was I. Theresa's bone marrow transplant was imminent.

CHAPTER FOURTEEN

Theresa was admitted to the hospital again on August 15. When I brought Theresa in that day, it was very difficult leaving her there. She knew that the chemotherapy she was about to receive would be even more intense than the first two rounds. The doctor had been quite precise in describing the side effects of the three different rounds of chemotherapies that would be administered to her. I look back at her courage and have to realize that she went through all of this in search of a permanent cure for herself, but she also tolerated it for her family. She didn't want to leave us because of "us." She also knew that she would be hospitalized for at least twenty-one days. She would be in isolation in very sterile conditions. Knowing that this would mean a long separation from Madison, who was now three years old, Theresa was very concerned. All of us were Gerald, his mom Mary, and I. Mary was tremendous during all of these months right from the beginning of Theresa's illness. She loved her as if she was her daughter and likewise we loved Gerald as a son. We always will.

Theresa had spent many hours preparing Madison for her absence. Except for her mommy's hospital stays, the two of them were definitely joined at the hip. They had always exchanged immeasurable affection.

We were particularly concerned about Madison not having Theresa to tuck her in at night, and about Theresa's absence in the mornings when Madison would awaken. Early morning was always one of their quiet times together--a gentle start to their days. They would cuddle while sitting on the sofa, and Theresa would stroke Madison's pretty hair or gently rub her back. She so loved that pampering.

I will have to say that for about the first week, every morning, Mary (Memom), and I would wonder "Whom will she want when she wakes up, and which one of us should keep her distance?" As we sat there having our coffee we would look at each other suspensefully.

Believe me, assertive Miss Madison would let us know whom and what she wanted, and there was no more suspense. Looking back, it really was somewhat comical. This little three-year old was so good at orchestrating the performances of her two grandmothers. I guess you could say Theresa should not have been concerned, as Madison had everything under control. Actually we were very fortunate that she had such good coping skills. She is a delightful child, and can bring such a large measure of joy to one's day.

Like her mom when she was a little girl, Madison was happy just to be outdoors. Pop Pop had built her a pretty neat sandbox complete with canopy. Theresa had insisted to her dad that Madison needed it, so of course he complied. She loved playing in it with all her toys. She would go from it, to her slide and swings, to her kiddy pool. She was content for the two of us to sit under the two grand oak trees in the backyard, she in her stroller and I on the crescent-shaped concrete bench. She'd pile her dolls, stuffed animals and blankets into the stroller and was as happy as could be. Sometimes I would read to her or sing to her, and other times she just wanted to hear about when mommy was a little girl.

Just about every day, we would have the boys across the street over and they would play together by the hour. The most special of her friends was Kyle, one of the cutest little redheaded boys you'd ever want to see. We had many a picnic on a blanket under those gorgeous oaks. Those were happy hours, time well spent.

Madison began settling into a routine. She had come to accept the fact that Theresa was going to be in the hospital for awhile. From August 15, up to and including August 24, Theresa had received very aggressive chemotherapy. During these nine days she experienced some very uncomfortable side effects from the chemo. The doctors and nurses did all they could to make her as comfortable as possible. On the tenth day she had no chemotherapy. Her body rested.

On August 26, 1995, Theresa's stem cells were returned to her. That was a long-awaited day. We were all so happy it had finally come, happy that all the chemotherapy was behind her. She called me after they had infused the stem cells into her through the port catheter and said, "Do you believe that it probably took all of fifteen minutes to have them go in?" It seemed ludicrous after all of the months of preparation it took to reach that point.

CHAPTER FIFTEEN

For several of the following days, as we had been forewarned, her condition was guarded. From having received all the chemo, her immune system was reduced to nothing. Her body had no ability to fight infection. We were very concerned at one point. Theresa had an extremely serious nosebleed in the middle of the night. The doctors and nurses had great difficulty stopping the bleeding. Her platelet count was very low. It was almost negligible. This meant that her blood had no coagulating capability. She could bleed to death. After several hours of being unable to arrest the nosebleed they packed her nose with gauze. She said it was extremely uncomfortable. She was given platelets several times. However, within a very short time of receiving them, her count would again become depleted. We were all frantic while this went on for about two or three days. I was beside myself. All I could think of was "What if she cannot produce platelets on her own?" We were all so concerned, so worried.

I began to feel numbness in my lips that would come and go. I also had a severe pain in the back of my head, on the left side of it. I didn't mention it to anyone. I thought it could be attributed to stress. However, the numbness continued and remained more constant and within a few days my mouth was asymmetrical. I couldn't eat or drink properly and my speech was somewhat slurred. I was having trouble forming my words. My face was becoming distorted, and my mouth drooped.

It was Gerald's day off. I hated to tell him about the way I was feeling. He already had so much to contend with. As soon as I told him he said, "Mom you should have told me when this started." We were unable to get an appointment with their family doctor since it was Labor Day weekend. He said, "I'll take you to a walk-in clinic." The doctor at the clinic diagnosed my condition as Bell's Palsy. He didn't prescribe anything but he told me to go home and get some rest. I would try to get an appointment with the family doctor on Tuesday.

That Friday, Saturday, and Sunday I didn't go in to see Theresa. I rested. The last thing she needed was to worry about me. On Labor Day I did go in to see her with Gale and Gwen. We had been at George's and Lynn's for a barbecue once again. I decided to go because it was unusual for me not to go in to see her. I didn't want her to become concerned. All visitors to the transplant unit had to wash their hands, wear a mask, gloves, a hat, a gown, and booties. As I said, she was being kept in very sterile conditions. How I still disliked the masks. However, the mask did serve the purpose of helping me to conceal from Theresa that I had Bell's Palsy. By now my left eye was blinking and watering incessantly. When she noticed my eye, I told her it must be an allergy. She couldn't see my face, so she was none the wiser.

Her doctor had determined what the problem was with her inability to make platelets. He discovered that there was an antibody that was eating up the platelets as fast as they were giving them to her and they must rid her of the antibody. He accomplished this by giving her an IV drug that corrected the problem. Her platelets started coming back. How relieved and thankful we all were. Theresa would remain in the transplant unit until they could see steady improvement in her blood counts.

I saw the family doctor on that Tuesday and she concurred that I did indeed have Bell's Palsy. She medicated me with steroids. Gradually the dosage would decrease. At her suggestion, I wore an eye patch at night when I went to bed. She was an excellent doctor. I felt very comfortable with her treating me. Now that I knew definitely what I was dealing with, I told Theresa. I got a good scolding for not telling her sooner.

A few days after Labor Day, her blood counts were sufficiently improved so that she could be moved back down to the second floor. They kept a close eye on her. She continued to improve and within a week or so was ready to be released.

Originally, the doctor had said that after Theresa's release from the hospital she would have to go to an inn near the hospital for an additional thirty days before she could go home. The reason for this was that she had little or no resistance to bacterial or viral infections. The plan was that I would stay at the inn with her, and Gerald would come by each evening so they could spend some time together.

Madison was due to start pre-school in September and obviously would be around other children. This could put her at risk to being exposed to bacterial or viral infections. Caution with Theresa had to be first and foremost as her immune system had been so drastically compromised. She, however, could not bear the thought of being apart from Madison for another thirty days. She, Gerald, and the doctor had a talk and they agreed to delay Madison's start to school until October. Theresa was so pleased with this decision. She would be able to go home upon her release.

We would still have to be very careful about infection. Before she came home the house had to be scrubbed from top to bottom. There could be no dust and we had to keep all surfaces as bacteria-free as possible, especially the kitchen and the bathrooms. Mary and I had started the cleaning procedure and Gerald hired a girl to come in and finish it. The house sparkled; it looked great.

I marvel at how Gerald was able to keep up with the demands on him during all those months. Their lives had been in such turmoil since that March but he was always encouraging, understanding, and remained a model dad and husband through it all. I feel that this must be said because some men, at times like these, just walk away. Theresa had met women along the way that this had happened to. It devastated them. She always felt truly blessed to have her Gerald, who must have been heaven-sent.

Madison's excitement was building. Her mommy was coming home. We made a beautiful poster with flowers on it that said, "Welcome Home Mommy" and we put it on the wall in a very prominent place where Theresa would see it when she walked in. She loved it and gave great praise to Madison. It was a big day and such a heartwarming sight to see the three of them together again. It was as it should be.

CHAPTER SIXTEEN

We were so thankful that Theresa had come through the transplant as well as she did. Now there would be additional weeks of recuperation and some new things for me to learn. She would need a daily infusion of Neupogen for one month. This procedure was necessary to help rebuild her bone marrow.

The home health care company, which had been providing all the medical supplies we had needed previously, (dressings, gloves, masks, etc.) would deliver this new drug to Theresa's home. They sent a visiting nurse to teach me how to administer the drug. It had to be given through the port catheter with the use of a battery-operated pump. I also had to learn the post-infusion care of the catheter line. At first I was very nervous about this new procedure but Theresa gave me a lot of reassurance and together we managed just fine.

She was on countless medications when she came home. Without a doubt, the only way I could keep an accurate record of her meds was to prepare daily charts with all the times, dosages and medications written down. I would check them off as I gave them to her. One cannot trust anything so crucial to one's memory.

She had side effects from some of the drugs. She was taking steroids. They made her feel on edge and very hungry but she was a good patient. She very rarely complained. She used to joke about both of us being on steroids. I was still taking them for the Bell's Palsy. Her observation was that we could become quite a pair what with the edginess and the hungry horrors.

Although she ate frequently, she couldn't really enjoy the food. The chemotherapy had temporarily destroyed her taste buds.

She also had to be on a neutropenic diet. There were a great many foods that were off limits to her. She could not have fresh fruits or uncooked vegetables. She couldn't have pepper, tap water, and many other things. These restrictions were placed on her diet in order to avoid bacteria.

As they had told her would happen, she did experience considerable bone pain from the Neupogen. At times it was almost unbearable. I can remember a number of occasions when the pain brought her to tears. At times like these, I'm sure she must have been feeling very discouraged. She had pain medication but disliked taking it as it upset her stomach so. I felt so helpless when the pain would become that severe. The mother in me just wanted to take the pain from her. The mother in me would have taken the disease from her but those choices are not up to us.

We made frequent trips to the clinic for follow-up visits. Every third or fourth day they would, as before, draw Theresa's blood to evaluate it. I must say that some of the most wonderful people in the medical profession are employed at John Dempsey Hospital at the University of Connecticut Campus in Farmington, Connecticut. People in every capacity were always so cordial, helpful and compassionate. It indicated to me that these employees had to be hand picked to preserve and maintain the high quality of care provided there.

As difficult as it had been for Theresa, Gerald, and Madison to go through all that they had since the previous March, I am so blessed to have been able to be there to help care for her. We always enjoyed each other's company so much but to know Theresa was to enjoy and love her.

We were now coming into October. I was still seeing the doctor for my Bell's Palsy. It was much better. By the third week in October, Theresa and Gerald felt they could manage on their own, so I came home. I know they were happy to have their lives back again and to have their home back to normal.

The whole experience had been an education for me and taught me how very delicate life is.

CHAPTER SEVENTEEN

It was good to be back home again. I had missed everyone a great deal but they understood my need to be with Theresa for as long as I had. Tom and I were pleased to be able to resume our normal routine. We lead a quiet life but it's a good life.

We talked to Theresa every day. Through October and November she was still having bone pain. Her walk had been rather stiff. I was really becoming very concerned. They were, however, able to come to our home for Thanksgiving. My mother was so happy to see them. She hadn't seen them since March. She doesn't travel well, so we couldn't take her to Connecticut, and of course the limitations put on Theresa made it impossible for her to come to Massachusetts.

We had a wonderful Thanksgiving and we were just that, "Thankful."

Through December the bone pain still persisted. The doctor reassured Theresa that it was all part of the process.

As was their custom, after Madison was born, they always stayed home on Christmas Day and would come to our home the day after and have Christmas with us.

Christmas of 1995 was very special as I look back in time. We should, none of us, ever take anything or any of our loved ones for granted. We must always keep our hearts open to each other.

The holidays being over, they began to think about going to Florida to visit Mary for three weeks. It was again off-season for Gerald. They always looked forward to this winter respite. They had planned to go in February but there was that bone pain still persisting.

Theresa was due to have her six-month scans. I could tell that they, as we, were very apprehensive about them. What a great relief it was when her scans came out showing no evidence of cancer.

They left on their trip. They went to Disney World for the first three or four days. Madison had breakfast with all of her favorite characters. She loved everything about Disney World, and Theresa and Gerald got such joy from being a family again. The trip did them a lot of good. Heaven knows they certainly needed the change. They had perfect weather, took in the beach almost every day, and enjoyed the time with Memom.

They came home in March. They all looked so refreshed. Theresa's hair was starting to grow back ever so slightly. Some of her eyebrows and eyelashes had also grown back. She was happy about that. It had been almost eight months since she had lost her hair after the first chemotherapy that previous May.

Gerald was more relaxed than I had seen him in months. He was so grateful to see Theresa on the mend and able to care for Madison again with relative ease. Life was good again!

CHAPTER EIGHTEEN

Easter would be coming soon and they would be coming to our home for the weekend. We would have a true reason to celebrate. We were all hoping that the Easter Bunny would bring a baby bunny for Madison along with lots of colored Easter eggs.

Easter morning arrived and Madison had a wonderful Easter egg hunt. She filled her basket. Then, there it was in its cage, the cutest black-and-white baby rabbit we had ever seen. Madison was beside herself. She couldn't believe her eyes. She named him Thumper. We love to go down to the barn to give carrots to him. When we do Madison looks at him and says, "He's just the sweetest little thing, Nana." She loves that bunny. He lives on our farm, so Pop Pop is in charge of his daily care.

We went to church. Theresa and Gerald got to see a number of people who were all interested in how Theresa was doing. Some were very surprised to see her there. I had gone back to the choir. It was a thrill for me that Easter morning to look down from the choir loft and see the three of them downstairs. We got home from church and all enjoyed a wonderful dinner. It had been a special holiday, truly joyous.

After Easter they started planning for Madison's birthday. It was hard to believe that she was going to be four.

Diane, Mae, and Jill, Diane's roommate, and I went down to Connecticut for the birthday party. It was a gorgeous day. We took full advantage of the delightful weather and set up everything in the backyard. There must have been fifteen children there with their moms. The kids played all of the usual party games. There was a lovely young girl doing face painting. That was a big hit. There were party hats, favors, a variety of snacks, soda, a beautiful birthday cake, and ice cream. The biggest attraction of the day was the moonwalk that Theresa and Gerald had rented for the kids.

I used four rolls of film that day to mark the occasion. Theresa was so happy and seemed so re-assured about her health. I had taken a beautiful picture of her in an adorable wide-brimmed hat which she was wearing that day. Her smile just spoke the words, "I DID IT!" as in, I have lived up to the challenge. I guess we all shared that optimism. It was a wonderful moment captured forever.

Every time I looked at Theresa that day I was just so overjoyed to think that she had made so much progress. It had been a long process for her. She seemed filled with such happiness. I know I was. I felt very different from the way I had felt the previous year at Madison's party.

Gerald had made it a point to come home early from the golf course. He, and even Theresa, jumped around in the moonwalk with Madison and the other children. At Madison's urging I got into it. Try as I might, I could not stay on my feet in that contraption. I found myself lying down in it unable to gain enough balance to get up. The things we do to please our grandchildren. I was very happy to get out of it. All in all the day had been just about perfect.

In June the girls came to visit us. They stayed for two days. We had bought a swing set for Madison. She was in her glory when she saw it.

The weather was good. We got to enjoy the pool. Much to our amazement, Madison was now able to stand in the shallow end with her head above the water. My, how she had grown. She was so proud of herself for being able to walk back and forth from side to side.

Of course, we went and had some "beach pizza." We took Madison to the park and Theresa ran into some of her high school friends. It had been several years since they had seen each other. Some of the girls knew that she had been ill. They had their own homes and one or more children.

The girls had a chance to catch up with what had been going on in their lives since their schooldays.

Madison and I wore each other out as she tried every swing; slide, seesaw, and tire swing that she found the time to get on. She always enjoys the park and indeed keeps me busy. It was a good time for all of us.

The two girls made it back to Massachusetts again in July. We took in some of the events of Amesbury Days and had a lot of fun. We took Joshua with us to Kids Day at the park. That night the four of us went to a concert in the Millyard. The group performing was extremely good. Music is my cup of tea. I thoroughly enjoyed the evening. We all did.

It was late afternoon. Michael had stopped in after work. I was busy in the kitchen preparing dinner. I looked out the window and noticed that Theresa was down back near the barn talking to Michael. They were looking at the horses. Although I was about a hundred yards from them, I got the impression that they were having a serious conversation. In fact, I felt a little uneasy. Eventually they came back to the house and that feeling left me. We had dinner and a quiet evening.

The next day, Theresa went to visit one of her childhood friends, Diana. Diana had been very upset when she heard about Theresa having breast cancer back in 1995. After she found out about it, she came to see Tom and me. She cried so hard. This was prior to Theresa's transplant. We didn't even know at that point all that lay ahead of Theresa. Without question, that July 1996 visit meant a lot to both of them.

The following month, Theresa and Madison came home for Yankee Homecoming. This is an annual celebration which takes place during the month of August in Newburyport. It has always been a fun-filled week. We took Madison and Joshua that weekend to take in some of the events. The kids and I went for a rowboat ride but the biggest event for both of them was the pony rides. Joshua, however, decided that at ten years old he should have a ride on a horse, and that he did. Madison was delighted to ride a pony. We walked around and took in all that we could. Joshua and Madison watched a karate demonstration. They were fascinated by it. We had our fill of pizza, soda, and ice cream. I think the kids could have gone for a few more hours but I was tired and so was Theresa, so we came home.

They spent Monday with us. Pop Pop took the three of us out for a meal of seafood. That day we ran into a girl whose son Theresa had cared for at a preschool when she was in high school. They hadn't seen each other since Theresa was a teenager and now her own son was in his twenties. Theresa found it hard to believe that so much time had gone by and that so much had happened in her life. She had experienced great joy and deep turmoil over the years, and seemed to be at a point where she was overcoming her largest hurdle, her cancer.

As was her custom, Theresa started back to her home after lunch on Tuesday.

A few weeks went by, and as usual we talked to Theresa every morning on the phone. As far as we knew, she was doing all right.

CHAPTER NINETEEN

It was August 28, late afternoon. The phone rang. It was Theresa. There were those tears again. I dreaded to hear her speak. She said tearfully, "Mom, my cancer is back. It's in my liver and in my neck." I asked her what the doctor had said. She replied, "That I probably have about two months." She said the doctor told her if she would take more chemotherapy, it would not be curative but it might buy her some time. She said to me, "But what would the quality of that time be?" She told me there was a small voice inside her saying, "No more chemo." At that point, trying to absorb all of this, I felt as if Satan had entered my body. I could not speak. I was writhing with noises I cannot even describe. It was as if I had to drive this shock from my body and I could only force it out with these sounds. It seemed as if minutes had passed. Finally being able to speak, I said "Theresa, I will have to call you back."

Tom was on the sunporch. He came in to see what was wrong. I told him and, oh, how we clung to each other in tears and utter disbelief. I thought, "Oh, my God, what will we do? How would we bear it? Our poor little girl, God help us. We had to save her. She had to live. Gerald needed her and Madison needed her. We just must save her."

Tom and I calmed and comforted each other. We regained some degree of composure. Immediately, I thought about a segment that I had taped from Dateline just a few nights prior. The piece was a report on a new experimental drug, which reportedly holds promise for some breast cancer patients. The drug is called HER-2 (her-2). The subject patient of the report was improving and her cancer did in fact go into remission with the drug treatment as I discovered some time later. That piece had aired just a few days before Theresa's devastating call. There was no immediate need for me to record it at that point, but I did. I placed the videocassette in my desk and thought if I ever need this in the future I'll have it.

In retrospect, little did I know that back in July when I had that uneasy feeling while watching Michael and Theresa down near the horses that my instincts were almost prophetic.

I mustered enough courage to call Theresa back. She said, "Mom are you all right?" She was concerned about me! How special she was.

I immediately tried to give her hope. I told her about the Dateline program and the HER-2. I assured her that I would start looking into it the first thing in the morning. We talked a bit longer. I asked her about Gerald. She put him on the phone but we could barely speak to each other. How my heart went out to him and his very precious girls. We agreed that none of us was about to give up on Theresa.

I could not go to bed that night. I lay on the sofa with the light on. I couldn't bear to close my eyes. My thoughts, my visions, were more than I could stand. I was having my worst nightmare and I was awake. What would become of Madison and Gerald? How would Theresa face her mortality? How would she ever come to grips with the possibility that she might forever leave them? I just couldn't turn my thoughts off. I cried, I prayed, I cried, I prayed, and finally I slept.

CHAPTER TWENTY

When I awoke the next morning I went through the process of assimilating it all again. How I wished it was only a bad dream.

Tom and I talked while we had our coffee and then we called Theresa. She sounded better, emotionally. I told her I'd get started on the inquiries about the HER-2 and that I would call her when I had more to tell her.

I played the Dateline videotape over and over and gathered as much information as I could from it. I tried to stay focused on the positive. We had to be positive, enthusiastic and supportive of Theresa and Gerald.

I started making phone calls. I called the pharmaceutical company in San Francisco, which was referenced on the tape. I explained Theresa's situation to the person on the phone. She gave me information on the drug and on the locations where clinical trials were in place for HER-2 in the Northeast.

I called Theresa again and told her of my conversation with the drug company representative. She said she was going to be in touch with a herbalist to see what he recommended as natural alternative treatment to combat the enemy within her vulnerable body. Ultimately, he developed a regimen of herbs, vitamins, minerals, and special select foods she should be eating. He also advised her of some of the foods she should avoid. She came to have great confidence in him.

After talking with her, I started to call the various hospitals whose names had been provided to me by the drug company representative. I found that under the protocols that were in place, Theresa would be required to have chemotherapy with the HER-2. In addition, the drug would be randomized. Which meant that instead of receiving the HER-2, she could receive a placebo. Those were the facts. Therefore, even if she agreed to chemotherapy, she might or might not get the HER-2. She didn't have the time to wait and see. There were different protocols, but each protocol required chemotherapy. They were structured so that if the patient's disease showed progression after three rounds of chemotherapy, which would be a round every three weeks, with the HER-2 every fourth week, (randomized) then they would discontinue the chemo and definitely put the patient on the HER-2 alone, guaranteed.

Remember, Theresa was told she had two months to live without chemotherapy, but there was that small voice saying "No more chemo."

That Saturday Diane, Mae, and I went down to see Theresa. I was so anxious to see her. She greeted us at the door with that beautiful smile of hers. It was as if a calm had fallen over both of us when we saw each other that day; neither one of us cried. Mae and Diane took Madison out to the yard to give us some time to talk. We talked realistically about what might happen. Theresa expressed to me that she wanted to be sure that her dad and I would maintain continuity in Madison's future. She said it was very important to her. She said she wanted us to give Madison what we had given her, our love. What a beautiful sentiment for a parent to hear from their child, and how beautiful a heart one's child must have to feel that. I assured her that Madison would always be a very important part of our lives and we would do our best to be the same in hers. We needed that time together. It was good for both of us. Diane was so considerate to have brought me down to see her.

Nina stopped by that day. She's always a ray of sunshine. We told her about the HER-2. She thought it sounded very promising.

Mae and Diane had come in when Nina arrived. We turned our focus to other things. Actually it had been a very nice visit. We left for home late afternoon.

Monday morning I called Theresa. She was still wrestling with the decision about the chemotherapy. She said she felt if she took more chemo she "would surely die." The memories of how she felt after the chemo prior to the transplant were all too vivid. The doctors assured her that the chemo would not be as bad as before but still she refused. I told her it was her decision and we would respect it, for it was, after all, her body. Gerald also was very supportive of Theresa's wishes.

I knew I must pursue a protocol without chemo. I was sure one existed, as the Dateline piece indicated that the patient on the program was receiving just the drug and there were no side effects as with chemotherapy (no nausea, no vomiting, no hair loss). The patient had received standard chemotherapy as part of her treatment after she had had a mastectomy in 1992. Some years later the disease reappeared and the progression was affecting her lymph nodes and her lungs. She and her husband had been searching for an alternative treatment to chemotherapy. Fortunately, for her, she was put into a clinical trial with HER-2.

Additionally, in order for a patient to be eligible to take this drug the patient would be required, through lab tests, to determine that her cancer overexpressed the HER-2 antibody. If, after the tests, the patient's blood and tumor did not overexpress the antibody, she would not qualify for this treatment. About one third of women with breast cancer have the HER-2 antibody, a molecule which fuels cancerous growth. It makes the disease more rampant than if a woman's cancer does not overexpress it.

Theresa had the appropriate testing and she did indeed overexpress HER-2. It was like a curse and a blessing at the same time; a curse in that it made the cancer so aggressive, and a blessing that she could avail herself of the anti-HER-2 drug treatment.

After a great many phone calls as an attempt to get the drug without chemo, the pharmaceutical company finally gave me a phone number to call for an expanded access program. I placed the call and told the girl who answered about the situation and that I wanted the HER-2 released to Theresa on a compassion basis. Much to my delight there was such a protocol in place. However, there were only two sites in the East where she could get the HER-2 alone. One was in Hershey, Pennsylvania and the other was in Rochester, New York. I called the Chamber of Commerce in Rochester and was informed that Rochester was 337 miles from Hartford, Connecticut. Theresa and Gerald lived about twenty miles from Hartford.

I still persisted in trying to get the protocol for Theresa closer to her home. Try as I might, I could not get the HER-2 released from the drug company on compassion except for the original two places I had been informed of, Rochester and Hershey. I had been pursuing the compassion protocol for thirteen days since August 29, except for weekends. I still have the journal in which I recorded every call that I made, along with the results of each call.

Feeling sure that there were no alternatives for Theresa, I spoke with the contact person in Rochester, New York on September 11. Her name is Ann Sass. I liked her immediately. She is a very warm, caring person. We talked at length and she concluded that Theresa should call her to arrange for an appointment.

Theresa placed a call to Ann. She also found her to be very informative and helpful. They talked and went over Theresa's history, and she made her appointment for September 23, 1996. We were relieved and filled with renewed hope. Could this drug hold the promise of life for Theresa?

CHAPTER TWENTY ONE

We knew that she would be in Rochester for two, maybe three, days on the first trip. Therefore, Theresa and Gerald decided that I would go with her. They didn't want both of them to be away from Madison for two nights. Memom would take care of Madison while Gerald was at work.

After Theresa was re-diagnosed and the news started to spread among family members and friends, she was on the phone for what to her seemed constantly. Everybody who heard it could not believe it. They were so concerned and all wanted to know what they could do.

As I told you early on, there are several young couples who are there for each other through good times and bad. Believe me they were there for Theresa and Gerald. They were fantastic. They prepared meals for them, helped to keep Madison occupied, and they prayed. There was such an outpouring of prayer from so many wonderful people. It was a much-needed source of strength for all of us.

In the meantime, while we were waiting for September 23, to come, Theresa's friend Colleen called me. The girls had kept in touch so she knew what had been going on with Theresa's health. She said she had been told about an organization, which flies patients all over the New England area for treatment, and she thought the cost would be minimal. Obviously the expense of Theresa's flying commercially each week would have been a huge financial burden, combined with all that they already had to cope with in terms of expenditures. Colleen gave me the number. I called and the secretary, Kitty, answered, "Angel Flight." I identified myself and began to tell her about Theresa. She was very compassionate when she heard about Theresa's condition, family status, and prognosis, and expressed such distress at Theresa's young age of thirty-four. Before she gave me any details about Angel Flight she said, "I will put Theresa's name into my prayer group immediately." I was most grateful, as prayer had carried us so far. She then told me that Angel Flight would fly Theresa at no charge for as long as she would need to be transported.

This organization is made up of pilots, some of whom own planes. They donate the use of their planes, the fuel, their time, and flying skills out of humanitarian concern. I say "humanitarian" but in my heart I feel that these very special people are indeed "Angels." Their organization is appropriately named.

Angel Flight of New England was then based in Beverly, Massachusetts, at Beverly Municipal Airport. It was about a half-hour from where Tom and I live. There are also other chapters of Angel Flight throughout the country. It is my understanding that they are able to network to assist patients, and their families who must travel beyond the areas covered by their particular chapters.

Kitty told me that if I ever wanted to accompany Theresa on a flight, I could leave with the pilots from Beverly and we would stop in Connecticut at Bradley International Airport to pick up Theresa and then fly on to Rochester. I saw this as such a generous gesture. What a great relief this would be to Theresa and Gerald. I called her to tell her what I had found out, and she was amazed at all that I had to report to her from my conversation with Kitty. She said, "It's like a gift from heaven," and it was.

CHAPTER TWENTY TWO

We decided that for the first appointment on September 23, we would fly on a commercial airline, as we would be gone for three days. Colleen, God bless her, got us two tickets at a very reduced rate and then refused to take the money for them, but that's Colleen.

Tom and Michael took me to Connecticut. Theresa had prepared a lovely lunch and Madison was delighted about having Pop Pop and Uncle Mike there. She was so excited that I would be staying overnight and thrilled that I had agreed to sleep with her.

Theresa and Michael had a chance to talk. I'm sure it must have been quite emotional for both of them. Even though separated by miles their hearts were very closely joined. Tom and Michael left for home mid-afternoon with great hope that the HER-2 was what could potentially put Theresa into remission. We all felt optimistic and remained very prayerful.

That night I slept with the wiggle worm. That is always eventful. She likes to sleep horizontally.

We got up at 4:00 a.m. on the twenty-third. Gerald got us to the airport at about 6:00 a.m. Our flight was scheduled for 7:05 a.m. When we went to check in I couldn't find my license. They needed a photo ID. Being unable to find the license, I became so agitated. How could I not have it with me? Finally I found it in a place where it should not have been. Theresa just looked me and said, "I don't know, Nanc." On occasion she would call me Nanc and call her father Tom. It was amusingly pleasing and appropriate in the spirit with which she did it.

After we got through the license episode we sat and talked as we were waiting to board the plane. I was most grateful to be accompanying Theresa.

We arrived in Rochester at 8:25 a.m. We picked up our luggage and then proceeded to rent a car. We went out for a bite of breakfast. We couldn't check into the hotel until afternoon. We had some time on our hands, so we first located Rochester General Cancer Center. Then we took a ride to Lake Ontario since it was only about fifteen or twenty minutes away. It was a bright sunny day. It was beautiful there. We spent a little time taking pictures and just admiring the awesome views of this huge body of water, and its surroundings. We enjoyed our time together.

When we arrived back at the Cancer Center we met Ann Sass, the contact person. She is a person with whom you feel very secure. She again went over Theresa's history with her and then the doctor came in to meet with her to evaluate her condition. She felt that Theresa was about ninety percent functional and should tolerate the treatment without a problem. Except for the stiffness in her neck she had been feeling quite well. Theresa had lab work performed, a chest x-ray, and a liver scan.

The next day was the "BIG DAY." We went in for her first treatment. She sat in the chair in the treatment room and I watched the nurse hook up the IV. On the IV pouch was written HER-2. As I looked at it I had an overwhelming feeling of relief. I felt as good about this drug as I had felt distressed back in 1995 when Theresa had her first chemo.

Theresa was smiling and happy. I was sure we had found our answer to saving our very precious daughter.

A little while after she was hooked up to the IV they brought some lunch to her. I went into the chapel just down the hallway. I wanted to give thanks for her being there. There was a journal available in the chapel that anyone was welcome to write in. Each time I went with Theresa, I wrote in it. It seemed important to write down my thoughts and what was in my heart.

I went back to the treatment room and sat with Theresa while she continued to receive the HER-2. The nurses were very congenial, so genuinely caring. After the treatment, she had to stay for an additional hour during which the nurse would check her vital signs every twenty minutes. After she was assured that Theresa was fine we were able to leave. The nurses all told her that they would look forward to seeing her the following week. The feeling was mutual. She was definitely filled with enthusiasm.

It had been a long day for both of us but especially for Theresa. When we went back to the hotel room she felt achy, almost as if she was coming down with the flu. I had brought a thermometer just in case she developed any side effects. Ann Sass had given us a list of possible mild ones, which might occur, such as fever. As Theresa napped, I was very nervous wondering how she would feel when she woke up. She slept until about 7:00 p.m. Upon awakening she said she felt a little better. I was relieved but still apprehensive about the night ahead. We watched some TV and relaxed. We both called home.

During the evening we had a chance to talk and shared our feelings of joy and optimism with each other. Our hopes were so high. Theresa had such resolve. She was determined to beat the cancer. Hopefully, the drug would arrest progression of the liver cancer and maybe even shrink some of the existing tumors. We so prayed that she would be as fortunate as the woman on Dateline.

Even though Theresa was so involved with fighting her disease, along the way she found time to reach out to other people. Back in October of 1996, she had agreed to be interviewed for a television health segment report, which would be aired on the Channel 8 Evening News out of Hartford. Gerald also appeared in the interview. It was a good report. We were so proud of them for their courage and their willingness to participate as an outreach to families facing similar situations.

Many people were already aware of her battle with cancer. Part of this was largely due to a newspaper report that had appeared in the *Hartford Courant* back in May of 1995. The reporter on the story was Nancy Thompson. The article told of Theresa's illness, her difficult decision about the bone marrow transplant, the incident with Saint Theresa, her patron saint, her dispute with the insurance company, and the fund-raiser.

Nancy did another very moving article after Theresa had been re-diagnosed. In that piece Nancy reviewed Theresa's history from the onset of the cancer to its recurrence, the HER-2 treatments and Angel Flight. Theresa was quoted in that piece as saying "People need to keep praying and relying on their faith to get through these tough times. Dateline helped me. I want to reach out to somebody, any hopeless case, and let them know there are alternative drugs out there and encourage people to get them."

Dateline had impacted Theresa's life so much. It was the vehicle through which she had gotten the tremendous renewed hope that we all shared in. When I was making my initial inquiries about the HER-2 I had called the producer of the segment, Tim Gorin. He wasn't available at the time but he was kind enough to return my call. He didn't have to do that but I truly respect him for having done so.

In November of 1996 Theresa was featured in a very informative article in the *Democrat and Chronicle Times* in Rochester, New York. It was National Breast Cancer Month and Theresa was asked if she would be willing to be interviewed. She of course agreed. Her feeling was that maybe she could help someone else to expand his or her horizons for combating the disease, whether that person was the patient or a member of the patient's family. The disease reaches out and devastates patient, family and friends. Having experienced this firsthand, Theresa could empathize and sympathize with other people who were in the midst of fighting a life threatening illness. She would give all she could.

The American Cancer Society had been very helpful to us during the course of Theresa's illness. I called them many times with questions about clinical trials, which might be in place for breast cancer patients. Each representative I spoke with always allowed me as much of her time as I needed. They mailed information to us on several occasions. It gives one great moral support to be able to access information, and can also provide a measure of hope when you need it so badly.

CHAPTER TWENTY THREE

The following week Gerald went to Rochester with Theresa. This would be their first trip with Angel Flight, a truly momentous occasion. They picked up Theresa and Gerald at Bradley and they were on their way. Their pilot was Spence. He would fly them several times. Theresa thought the world of him. He went so far as to arrange for a van to transport them to and from the hospital. Gerald was happy to be there with Theresa. Her second treatment went well. The staff at Rochester General was outstanding. They were always so warm and friendly.

While Gerald and Theresa were in New York that day, Kitty from Angel Flight called me. She said that they had received a call from "Chronicle" of Channel 5 in Boston. Chronicle is an evening newsmagazine that covers a multitude of subjects. It is a very informative program. It has been on the air, I believe, since 1982. That speaks to its reputation and endurance in the very competitive world of television broadcasting.

Kitty wanted to know if Theresa would be willing to allow Chronicle to accompany her on her next trip to Rochester. She also wanted to know if I would be willing to participate and fly from Beverly so that they could give an in-depth view of just what Angel Flight can do for families. I said I couldn't guarantee what Theresa would say but I thought that as long as she felt well enough she would be willing to do it and so would I.

She did feel all right after her second treatment and without hesitation did agree to participate in the TV coverage for Chronicle.

This would be quite an experience for both of us but most importantly it would be a wonderful opportunity for the public to be informed about Angel Flight. There is such a need existing for this kind of help, and most people don't even know about this organization.

Tom and I left home that morning at 5:15. I was very nervous about flying but anxious to see Theresa and very anticipatory about the Chronicle piece. We arrived at the Beverly Airport about 6:00 a.m. It was still pitch dark out and it was foggy. We could see a light in the office and we then observed some activity. We went in and met Larry Camerlin who is the president of Angel Flight. Immediately, we could see that this was a very special man. We met Kitty. It was nice to meet her as I had spoken with her so many times on the phone. There were several people scurrying around, and Tom and I tried to figure out what each person's function was. It was an interesting experience. Larry announced that he had made arrangements for a large plane to accommodate all of us.

The pilot, Charlie, was a great guy and a super pilot. Charlie got involved with Angel Flight quite by chance. He was at the airport one day in their office when Kitty and Larry got a call about a young boy with leukemia who needed transportation. He was from Maine. Charlie spoke up and said he would be happy to do the flight. What motivated him, as he told me, was sheer gratitude for his young son having survived a life-threatening illness some years earlier. This was one small way, Charlie said, of paying back for his son's miraculous recovery. Charlie told me that out of twenty-eight hospitals all over the country that he and his wife had been to, only three of them had given them any hope for their infant son. He said, "So don't ever accept it when somebody tells you there is no hope, always keep looking, never give up." I said, "We won't."

Charlie and Larry were waiting for the fog to lift. Daylight had come but conditions were such that we couldn't take off. I called Theresa to tell her we would be delayed. We sat in Kitty's office and Ken the videographer from Chronicle shot a segment from there and then went outside with Charlie and Larry to the plane to shoot more footage. After the fog had lifted sufficiently we got clearance to take off. Larry gave all of us headsets so that we could hear the communication from the tower. It was a new experience for me and I found it quite fascinating.

The interviewer from Chronicle, Dick, was accompanying Ken as the second half of their two-man team. They were both very pleasant. They were the kind of people you felt you had known forever.

We talked about Theresa and her family, about their work for Chronicle, and about Angel Flight. It only took about 45 minutes to get to Connecticut. Theresa said good-bye to Gerald and Madison and walked out to the plane. I was so happy to see her. She looked good and said she felt good.

At that point she had gone through ten radiation treatments on her neck. She had the radiation at the University of Connecticut Health Center where she had had her bone marrow transplant. She had such respect for all of the people there. They were always very good to her. The radiation had helped relieve the pain and stiffness in her neck. We were pleased about that and now she would get the third HER-2 treatment.

She talked at great length with Dick and Ken. The day moved a little slowly because of the footage they were doing. They accompanied us in the van on the way to the hospital. Dick asked her some questions about her everyday battle and I was so moved by her reply. She said that she thought of every day as a "gift from God." She also said, "I have a four year old who needs me and that gives me a very good reason to get up each morning." She exuded such courage and determination.

We arrived at the hospital and the nurses were waiting for Theresa. They all wanted to know how she was feeling. They were always so uplifting. They started her treatment and brought some lunch to her. I went for a bite of lunch and then I made a visit to the chapel. I again wrote in the journal.

After Theresa's treatment, she had to wait for the usual hour to have her vitals checked. By the time we left the hospital and got back to the Rochester airport it was getting quite late. The bad weather was beginning to close in. However, Ken and Dick still wanted to do some footage on Charlie and Theresa before taking off. Charlie agreed. His contribution to the piece was great and so was Theresa's. I think we all felt that they could put together a good segment on Angel Flight for Chronicle with all the film they had shot that day.

Charlie was eager to get into the air and get us home safely.

CHAPTER TWENTY FOUR

We finally boarded the plane in Rochester, and headed for Bradley International Airport in Connecticut. The rain was torrential and the ride a little bumpy now and then. Theresa looked at me and asked, "Mom, are you all right?" I said, "I'm fine" and she replied, "I can't believe how calm you are." I told her I wasn't nervous because "God was sitting between us." She smiled that unforgettable smile. A short time later Charlie announced that we wouldn't be able to land in Connecticut as the weather was so bad he couldn't get cleared for landing. He said we would have to come directly to Massachusetts. That meant Theresa would come home with us.

Gerald was very concerned back in Connecticut because he was expecting us to land with Theresa. We were so delayed he began to inquire about why we hadn't arrived yet. The tower at Bradley told him they couldn't verify the whereabouts of our plane. He and Tom had been talking on the phone.

They were both thinking that our plane had gone down. They were frantic!

In the meantime, Charlie and Larry announced that we weren't going to be able to land in Beverly either, conditions were too foggy.

When we left Rochester and the weather was closing in, Charlie had said there was nothing to worry about as we had five and one-half hours of fuel on board. He continued to look for alternative places to land and it necessitated our flying around for a substantial amount of additional time. I think we had been in the air for close to four hours and I started thinking about the five and one-half hours of fuel we left Rochester with. I was very relieved when he announced that we were cleared for landing at Hanscom Air Force Base in Bedford, Massachusetts. He landed the plane and its passengers beautifully. He's an excellent pilot. We felt safe with him.

The rain was still coming down so fast and so heavy. The runway took on the appearance of one huge puddle. They sent a van out to us and drove us to the terminal. Theresa and I immediately went to the phones. She called Gerald and I called Tom who, at this point, was beside himself, as was Gerald. They certainly breathed sighs of relief when they heard from us. We all went by taxi to Beverly. When we arrived Tom was there waiting. He was overjoyed to see us one and all.

Dick, the interviewer, had been quite nervous during the flight. I fully expected him to kiss the ground when we got back to Beverly. We said our good-byes to everyone we had spent the day with and headed for home. We were exhausted. We hadn't eaten since lunch so Tom stopped at a diner on the way home and we had some supper. It was still raining torrentially. Even the driving was bad. It had been a very long day for everyone. We arrived at our home around 10:00 p.m. and turned in for some much deserved rest.

The next day we took Theresa home. In fact, she drove. She said she felt fine and insisted on driving. When we arrived, Madison was thrilled to see her and us.

The next two weeks, Gerald went to Rochester with Theresa. Spence flew them. She looked forward to seeing him. All seemed well. She felt good.

CHAPTER TWENTY FIVE

We began to think about Theresa's flights for the upcoming winter. Angel Flight does not have a plane of its own that is equipped with a de-icing device. We wanted to try to do something for them. They had been so good to us. I wrote a letter to a popular talk show host in hopes of getting a reply. I knew that there could be a wonderful show done on Angel Flight. My letter suggested that the program could focus on the tremendous good done for people by Angel Flight. There are so many people in need of transportation to their treatment sites, which can come at such a high price. Additionally, I thought an appeal might be made to corporations to donate a corporate jet or a twin engine plane which would be equipped to fly in the winter elements. With Theresa's courageous fight against this cancer, there was a good story to be told here. There are thousands of families fighting this disease or other dire illnesses.

Regrettably, I never received an answer to my letter. We were quite disappointed. We so wanted to find a way to reciprocate to Larry and Angel Flight for all that they had done for us. I haven't given up hope. I know the show gets thousands of letters. Maybe, someday, a staff member will bring this idea to the forefront as a worthy subject.

In the meantime, a New England cable station wanted to do a piece on Angel Flight. It was National Breast Cancer Month and Larry called to see if Theresa and I would be willing to again participate in this particular program. Of course we agreed. Theresa wouldn't think of refusing as long as she felt well.

As we prepared for this next trip to Rochester, the weather again was terrible. We had rain with such force that many of the roads in our town were washed out and impassable. There was only one way out of town for us. When we left the house that morning at 4:30 a.m. we didn't know what was ahead of us. All we could do was pray that we would make it to the airport, but Tom was confident that we would. Thanks to his skillful driving we did. Larry met us and from there we drove to Hanscom Air Force Base. After we arrived, we waited for the health science reporter, Cara, and the videographer from the cable station.

For that flight we had another pilot with his own corporate jet. This young man, Alex, flies for several organizations. He transports patients to and from their treatment sites, and he also flies organs for transplant. He does all of these wonderful deeds as missions of mercy and compassion. It is strictly a labor of love for him, a remarkable human being.

Cara conducted an excellent interview with Theresa, Larry, Alex, and me. She also interviewed Theresa's doctor at Rochester General about the HER-2 clinical trial which Theresa was participating in. Theresa had indeed reached out to many other cancer patients and their families with the media exposure in which she took part. I hope all of her efforts made a difference to some.

Cara had done a marvelous job and, moreover, gave great focus to Angel Flight. She received an award from The American Cancer Society for the report. Subsequently, she became a reporter for the evening news on Boston's Channel 5, which is co-anchored by Natalie Jacobson and Chet Curtis. Obviously, she is very well accomplished.

Gerald accompanied Theresa on her other trips up to and including the seventh week. He enjoyed going with her and she loved having him there. He was her rock.

The nurses and other staff at Rochester General were excited at the prospect that the HER-2 could possibly help Theresa. All of them were praying for her and were so supportive.

We knew that when Theresa went for her eighth treatment she would have another liver scan. They had told her that if the disease had progressed over the eight-week period, they would discontinue the HER-2 treatments.

We were optimistic and apprehensive at the same time. So much depended on the results of that scan.

I went with Theresa because, as with the first time, it would be a two-day trip. Gerald wanted to stay with Madison to avoid too much upheaval for her. We flew commercially, and once again, Colleen gave us the tickets.

CHAPTER TWENTY SIX

This trip was so special, I decided to treat us with great accommodations. We checked into the Marriott in Rochester. It was lovely.

Theresa had to be at the hospital at 10:00 a.m. for the scan. I had lived in my mind over and over again what it would be like to get a good report. I must confess I also lived in my mind the other possibility. However, I always chose to dismiss that thought. We had to stay positive.

Theresa went in for the scan. She had brought in with her a small crucifix that had been given to her by my very dear friend Jean. It was small enough to be handheld. Theresa clutched at that cross for many hours during the course of her illness; it seemed a source of strength to her.

The time seemed to pass so slowly after she went in for the scan. I kept looking for her to come out. At last, she did. She asked the technicians to give her an indication of her results but they could not. They said they had to follow procedure and she would have to wait until the next day when she would see her doctor. Theresa was insistent about seeing her films. They informed the doctor of Theresa's strong need to know what the results had been. Her doctor gave them her consent and they gave them to her.

We brought them to a private room in the waiting area. We could see that there were several more tumors than there were when her treatment had begun. We were in shock and utter disbelief. This couldn't be happening. We hugged and cried and tried to comfort each other. I felt so helpless. Over the years whenever something went wrong her dad and I were always able to help and to fix whatever the problem was. This time was different. We couldn't fix it. The control of the situation was out of our hands, out of all of our hands except for God's.

We calmed down as best we could and left for the hotel. How we both dreaded going back. Gerald was waiting to hear from Theresa. He had been so filled with hope. Tom was waiting for my call.

It was November 11, 1996, the eighth wedding anniversary of Nina and George. It had been on November 11, 1988, that Theresa and Gerald had found each other again. How could one date have such opposite impacts on the lives of two such beautiful people?

Theresa was trying to prepare herself emotionally to call Gerald. She said, "Mom, why don't you call Dad?" I placed the call. It was definitely the most difficult thing I had ever had to do. He adored her. I said. "Hon, I'm sorry to tell you this but I don't have good news." He said, "Oh no." We were both very emotional and agreed that we would talk again later that day. I was so glad I was there for Theresa and so sad that I wasn't there for Tom.

Our dear daughter then proceeded to call Gerald. My heart broke for the two of them, so in love, so committed to each other, and to Madison, and here they were faced with the worst results they could have anticipated. I knew she just needed his arms around her so badly and he needed the same from her.

CHAPTER TWENTY SEVEN

What a long day and night it would be. Theresa's appointment with the doctor wasn't until the next morning.

I sat on my bed, she on hers, and we started to talk. I said "Theresa, I can't imagine starting my days without our morning phone calls." We always called each other a little after 8:00 a.m.

That three or four-minute phone call was such a big part of Tom's and my day. It just got us started off on the right foot. The daily phone calls were just that, "daily," from the time she had made her home in Connecticut with Gerald.

She said "I love you, Mom," got up and gave me a gentle hug and kiss on the cheek. She said, "I can't believe I'm going to die." Then she said tearfully, "My poor Gerald and my poor little girl, how will my little girl stand it without her mommy?" I had no answer for her. I couldn't fix it.

She so wished that she could just go home that day but she did have to see the doctor the next day.

We spent most of the day in our room. We talked some more, cried some more and strangely enough we found things to laugh about.

That night we decided to go down to the dining room to have a leisurely dinner. As I sat across from Theresa I said, "You just look so good." She shrugged her shoulders and said, "Go figure."

We talked about many things during dinner and we did enjoy the time together.

We went back to our room. Theresa called Gerald and Madison. She was so courageous when she spoke to Madison. She told her she was going to bring home a surprise to her for being such a good girl. She told her she loved her and couldn't wait to see her. My heart was shattered, so saddened. She and Gerald spoke again. She was very concerned about him.

We shared many more thoughts before turning in and surprisingly we both slept that night.

The next morning we got ready for her doctor's appointment. When we arrived at the hospital, the nurses who had been giving Theresa her treatments came over to us and hugged us. Some cried quietly with us and did their best to comfort us. Theresa had certainly touched their lives and above all she had touched their hearts. As I said before, she just had that way about her.

We could see that the doctor was very saddened to have to confirm Theresa's prognosis to her. She asked her to consider taking low dose chemotherapy when she returned to Connecticut but again Theresa said, "No."

Theresa then said to the doctor, "I want to go to Disney World with my daughter and my husband. Should I go before Christmas or after?" The Doctor replied, "Why don't you go before?" This told us, without being told specifically, that Theresa's condition would probably deteriorate fairly quickly.

The doctor expressed to Theresa how sorry she was that the drug had not helped her. She was sympathetic but professionally detached, as I am sure this is the only way that a doctor can cope with this monstrous disease. Thank God that doctors have some successes to sustain them. They are entitled to some happy moments to be shared with their patients.

Although the HER-2 didn't help Theresa, perhaps her participation and that of others who took part in the clinical trials for the drug will help to solve a small part of the puzzle. Patients who volunteer for these studies could be key to finding a cure for this horrendous illness.

Before we went back to the hotel, we went to a toy store and bought some surprises for Madison. Theresa had to keep her promise to her girl.

When we got back to our room we decided to try to arrange for a late checkout. The desk clerk said we could stay until 2:00 p.m. It worked out well for us. Our plane was leaving at 4:00 p.m.

We both called home again. Gerald was so anxious for Theresa to get home.

It had started to snow. We decided to order lunch from room service. We talked some more. Theresa had so many thoughts racing through her mind. I wondered if I should share some of my thoughts with her. She was so concerned about Madison and how she would cope with her mommy's death.

I decided to share with her what had been on my mind. I said, "You know, Theresa, small children are very resilient. Madison will miss you desperately but in time she will adjust." I told her I knew first-hand because my father had died when I was three. I said I didn't remember much about him but I always remembered being told what a wonderful man he was. My mother, her family, and my dad's family kept his memory alive for me. I said, "That is how it will be for Madison." I added "In my day we had no videos but there are many of the three of you and this will help her to maintain more vivid memories than I did of my dad and they will help her to see just how loved she was by you." I also told her that if Madison were a few years older it probably would be more difficult for her to accept.

Theresa was quiet for a while and then she said to me, "Thank you for telling me that, Mom, it makes me feel better about Madison."

Always putting the needs of her loved ones before hers, she told me, "I'm going to go home, make my funeral arrangements to make it easier on Gerald later on and when that's done, we're going to Disney World."

Looking back, as sad as most of those two days were for us, we also shared joys of times past. We reassessed our years together and concluded that the love and the bond that we shared were so special that they would never die.

To my dying day, I will always treasure those two days I spent with her. We cried, we laughed, and we expressed our love. It was so difficult on the one hand but so beautiful on the other, memories that no one can ever take from me. God was so good to grant us that time together.

CHAPTER TWENTY EIGHT

At 2:00 p.m. we checked out of the hotel. It was still snowing. When we got to the airport we had a little time on our hands. Theresa had found a chapel. We went in and we sat. We prayed together and again we cried together. Although the HER-2 had not been the miracle we had hoped for, we were still praying for a miracle. We vowed we would start looking for a new answer, a cure for Theresa. We left the chapel.

We boarded the plane and left for Connecticut. Theresa was eager to see Gerald and Madison. We had a pleasant flight. Even with this dark cloud hanging over her she was still a pleasure to be with. She was not bitter or angry. She was just focused on her family and wanting to enjoy them to the fullest.

When we arrived in Connecticut they were waiting for us. Madison was all excited to see her mom and inquisitive about her surprises.

Gerald greeted Theresa with a kiss, a hug, a smile, and optimism. He was not ready to accept anything other than that Theresa would beat this disease. They were both ready to continue the battle but Theresa kept her resolve to make her funeral arrangements. Gerald reluctantly agreed just to put her at ease and get it off her mind.

The following Sunday they were going to attend a healing service in Sturbridge, Massachusetts. Theresa invited me to go with them and their friend Linda. She used to work with Linda for Linda's brother, Stephen, who is a physical therapist. When Theresa became ill in 1995, after her mastectomy, she used to go to Stephen for treatment. He helped her a great deal, as did Linda.

I had called Colleen about the results of the HER-2. She was very upset and so concerned for Theresa, Gerald, and Madison. I told her about the healing service that coming Sunday and she said she would like to come with us.

Tom and I met Colleen in Peabody that Sunday and she drove us to Sturbridge. We had great conversation on the way. She is excellent company and such a caring friend.

We spotted Theresa and Gerald. They were both very upbeat just to be there. We made our way through the crowd and went into the room where the service would take place. The room was immense. There were twelve hundred people there and they were all seated on folding chairs in one room. It was a very impressive thing to see all those people gathered together. It would prove to be a very moving, and emotional experience.

The priest spoke to the crowd. I found him to be a dynamic speaker. At various intervals all of the people would sing beautiful hymns. It is said that when you sing the praises of the Lord it is like praying twice. The music added an extra spiritual dimension for me.

The priest then offered Mass. It was a beautifully moving celebration of the faithful.

After Mass, he began to address the crowd. Then he spoke to people with afflictions. He laid hands on some. We witnessed, first-hand, some very impressive experiences of healings on some of the people present. One young woman, who had been dependent upon her crutches to walk, actually walked without them. Another got up out of her wheelchair and walked, others in wheelchairs did not. One man who had a disease, which caused him to be terribly stooped over, went through a tremendous transformation. The priest spent a lot of time with him. He began asking him if he could raise his body a little and the man did. He asked several more times if he could rise up a little higher and each time he did he stood a bit taller. Ultimately, this man who initially appeared to be about five feet tall was indeed a very tall man, who was now standing as straight as an arrow. It was truly amazing to see God's healing working through this priest.

Never did the priest imply that he heals, he emphasized that he is God's instrument. He had discovered this strong connection and gift many years prior. He has traveled all over the country and to different parts of the world. He is tremendously respected and has a very large following.

While addressing the crowd he said that the night before at about 3:00 a.m. the name Nancy came to him and the disease associated with the name was breast cancer. He wanted to know if there was a Nancy with breast cancer in the crowd. He asked repeatedly and nobody stood. Finally, I told an usher that my name was Nancy and not I but my daughter had metastatic breast cancer. She asked us to come down to the front of the room with her. After we were there he began to ask for a girl named Theresa. He said, "She is here and she has endomytriosis and today she will be cured." Theresa didn't respond, as she didn't have the disease he was referring to. Other people, maybe twenty, were also at the front of the room. The priest would talk to them individually and anoint them. When he got up to us in the line the usher told him that I was Nancy and she said, "This girl's name is Theresa and she has breast cancer." He looked at her and said, "So you're Theresa." He anointed her, looked deep into her eyes and said, "Go home and see what happens."

It was almost unbelievable to us that out of twelve hundred people Theresa would end up being one of those anointed and prayed over.

We returned to our seats and we were all in awe of what had happened. Theresa, Gerald, and all of us were thrilled. We felt Theresa's miracle had occurred. Not only did we feel it we truly believed it. The experience had given her newfound hope.

The service which had begun at noon concluded at around 6:00 p.m. The time had flown by. Afterward we went out for dinner and reviewed the day, each from our own perspectives. We were all very happy.

CHAPTER TWENTY NINE

Thanksgiving was just around the corner. In the days following Theresa packed everything for their trip to Disney World. She was feeling good and they were looking forward to Florida. They all loved the warm weather and the ocean.

They came to our home the night before Thanksgiving. We had a pleasant family evening and the next day a wonderful holiday. They left late that afternoon and Friday they flew to Disney World.

Theresa called us from their hotel. She said it was like a wonderland. She told me about the Christmas tree that could be seen from their room. She described it as being about five stories high and absolutely breathtaking. She was as excited as Madison was. She sounded great. They had four fun-filled days at Disney World. They went on to Gerald's mom's house the following day. She was in Connecticut but the kids stayed at her home. Their plan was to come back on December 20, to get ready for Christmas.

For several days they would pack a lunch and spend most of their days at the beach. They were all loving it and having wonderful time.

While they were in Florida some of their dear friends, back home, knowing what probably was ahead for Theresa and Gerald organized a fundraiser for them. They did it in the form of a spaghetti supper. A lot of time and effort went into the planning and preparation of the event. It was amazingly well attended and this group of wonderful people managed to raise $10,000 for them. This was such an outpouring of love and support from this group and the community. It enabled Gerald to spend precious time at home with Theresa, and gave to both of them a tremendous feeling of financial security. As I said before, their friends are very special people.

While in Florida, Theresa started to experience discomfort in her back. She wasn't sure just what it was. At first it would come and go. Within a short period of time the pain got really intense. None of the over-the-counter pain medication seemed to touch it. They called her oncologist at the University of Connecticut Health Center. He wanted to see Theresa as soon as they got back. Her doctor was so good to her. She had great confidence in him and felt secure being in his care.

At that point I told Theresa that I had saved a newspaper article from January of 1996. It was about a doctor who was working on an immunotherapy. It is administered inter-dermally and has few, if any, side effects. I made several phone calls to the lab where the research was being conducted. I told them about Theresa and they said they would need specimens of her blood to determine how her shots should be formulated. Every patient's chemistry is unique and must be treated accordingly. Theresa's oncologist was agreeable to her receiving the immunotherapy if she so desired. I felt after researching the therapy that this approach to fighting cancer had great potential. I was very optimistic about its ability to possibly conquer the disease in Theresa.

I spoke with one patient who had been declared terminal before she started the therapy. Her cancer was in her bones. It was so advanced, she had holes in her pelvis. She chose to take the therapy as a last resort for a hope of saving her life. When I spoke with her she told me that after several months on the therapy she had been scanned that past July of 1996 and there was no evidence of metastatic disease in her body. I was so encouraged, so confident. I conveyed this information to Theresa. She, too, found it encouraging.

As the days passed Theresa's pain had become almost unbearable. They decided to come back from Florida a day early on the nineteenth. On the twentieth she saw her doctor who ordered a bone scan. The scan revealed that she had a tumor in her spine. She would need radiation treatments to try to shrink the tumor and stop further spreading of the cancer. That day, December 20, 1996, Theresa had her blood sent to the immunotherapy laboratory for evaluation.

She was scheduled to start the radiation. They told her that it would relieve the pain after six or seven treatments. Needless to say, Christmas wasn't a joyous time for them or any of us.

Theresa's pain continued to intensify. Poor Gerald felt so helpless and was doing everything humanly possible to help her and try to make her comfortable. He was very good about keeping us informed every evening about how Theresa's day had been. The doctor was trying to determine the best pain medication for Theresa but everything he tried was harsh on her stomach and she became unable to hold down any food.

After the first of the year she was admitted to the hospital. She was dehydrated, getting very weak and the pain was still unbearable.

We decided to go to Connecticut for a few days. We were so happy to see her and she to see us. It was very difficult seeing our "little girl" in that hospital bed. They had her very heavily medicated. When we walked in she said, "Gee, Mom and Dad, you both look about three feet tall," and she chuckled. We had our delayed Christmas with them the next day in her hospital room. As happy as we were to be together, it was bittersweet.

Within the next two days she began to be able to eat small amounts of food. She continued to have the radiation treatments while in the hospital. All of the nursing staff was absolutely wonderful to her. They did all that was humanly possible to make her comfortable. In the interim she began her immunotherapy. This therapy is intended to boost the immune system and, unfortunately, the radiation surpresses the immune system. One was fighting the other. The thought of this was greatly distressing. We just wanted the radiation to be completed. The day of her last radiation treatment they released her from the hospital. We were pleased that it was behind her.

Now, maybe the shots would have a chance to work.

CHAPTER THIRTY

The doctor had put her on a new regimen of pain medication along with prescriptions to control the nausea and vomiting. As she settled into being back home again the pain still persisted. It wasn't as severe as it had been in December but it was still there. They kept waiting for the radiation to "kick in" and bring the relief that she needed so badly.

With the pain continuing over the next couple of weeks, her doctor decided that he should do another scan. The scan showed no new cancer. He wasn't satisfied. He was looking for an explanation for the pain. He ordered another bone scan. That scan showed another tumor on her spine. Two of her discs were so compressed they were resting on each other. The doctor decided she must have more radiation. So there she was, needing ten more radiation treatments. She continued the immunotherapy treatment.

We still held out a lot of hope for when she would finally be done with the treatments so that the new therapy could work. In February she finished her radiation. She started to feel somewhat better. She had developed some difficulty with walking comfortably. She walked slowly and cautiously. Each step seemed very deliberate. Her walk was quite stiff. We were concerned about it, but we felt she just needed to give it some time.

Her color was good, her eyes were clear and bright, her appetite was improving and she was spending much more time out of bed with Gerald and Madison. She was having no problems with her liver, at least none that she knew of on a day-to-day basis.

Gerald had been off from work for the winter months. It was good that he could spend the time with Theresa and Madison. Thank God and all those wonderful people for that spaghetti supper.

Things reached a point where Theresa announced one day that she would like to go for a ride. They were all so delighted that she felt up to it. Things seemed to be looking up. We marveled at her resilience. They started going out more. They even managed to go out to dinner on their anniversary on February 17. It had been seven years since they had taken their marriage vows. They had Madison, the beautiful gift of their love, and they were again filled with hope. Theresa was still receiving the immunotherapy.

Obviously, she had not been to our home since Thanksgiving. We were all hoping that maybe by spring they would be able to come for a visit. Her grandmother was especially hoping for that. She was now 85 and derived such pleasure from Theresa and her family.

Theresa's illness had been a very difficult thing for her to deal with. She never complained about its effect on her but I could see it in her eyes and in her face. She has always been a very strong woman. As I mentioned earlier, my father died when I was three. My mother was only twenty-eight. He was thirty-six. Twenty-eight years old was a very young age at which to become a widow.

We were alone for the next eight years. She worked very hard to make a good home for the two of us. I spent a great deal of time, in my formative years, with my grandmother because of my mother's necessity to work. She was one of the sweetest souls God ever created. I am truly thankful that my mother and I had her. We were greatly blessed by the care, and love, which she so willingly gave to us.

My mother remarried when I was eleven. My stepfather was a wonderful man. I was happy about their marriage. He gave us a good life.

They were thrilled when Tom and I started our family. Family was always our focus, all of us, and it still is.

At any rate, my mother was looking forward to Theresa's recovery and was so anxious for the day when she would see the three of them again.

In March, when we would talk to Theresa, in the mornings, she sounded a little short of breath. When I asked her about it she said, "I don't know if it's my liver or if I'm retaining fluid. The doctor is going to scan me."

How we prayed that she would get a good report. She had been taking the immunotherapy now for about two months. We were looking for improvement in her liver or, at least, that the scan would show no more involvement than had her last scan in Rochester back on November 11. We eagerly awaited the call from her and Gerald to see what was going on with her liver and her breathing. Much to our disappointment there were more new tumors on the liver. We still could not give up hope.

Some days her breathing was better than other days. Eventually she started to feel more pressure on her lungs from her liver. It was very enlarged and her abdomen was greatly distended.

At this point Theresa's doctor talked to her again about chemotherapy. She agreed to have it as she was having so much discomfort. She was still trying to hold on, for herself, and also for all of us.

CHAPTER THIRTY ONE

At this time we had heard about a new clinical trial using a drug that cut off the blood supply to tumors, thus, ultimately the tumors would die. In theory this sounded like another possibility for Theresa's recovery or at least for management of her cancer.

I began looking into whether there were any clinical trials in place for breast cancer patients. I made contact with the pharmaceutical company and found two sites in Virginia. A pre-requisite to being eligible for the trial was that the patient must have six rounds of the chemo drug Adriamycin to qualify for enrollment in the trials. We were all very grateful that she might have a new chance at life. It brought me back to the day when Charlie, our pilot, had said to me, "Don't ever accept it when somebody tells you there is no hope, always keep looking, never give up."

Periodically, I used to talk to Angel Flight's Larry Camerlin about Theresa. I told him about the possibility of Theresa going to Virginia for treatment. He told me that whenever she was ready to let him know and Angel Flight would fly her there. He also told me that if we ever wanted to get to Connecticut quickly he would fly us down. He is truly a prince among men, a gift to mankind.

March was coming and Gerald was going to have to return to work. Although I had offered to go down through the winter and stay to help out, they wanted to keep things as normal for Madison as they could. I respect them so much for that. For all that they were both going through their mutual main concern was their dear little girl, such an unselfish young couple.

They decided that I would come down in March to stay and care for Theresa but they wanted a Nanny for Madison. They had help from friends trying to guide them in the right direction. They interviewed a few girls and then they interviewed Cathy. They both decided that it would be this girl who would care for Madison. She had come very highly recommended and provided excellent references. Having made this decision was a great relief to both of them.

Therefore, the plan was that I would go down for March 26, so that Gerald could return to work full time on that date.

Over the winter we had gotten down about every other week to see them. Each time, Theresa appeared to be holding her own but now this breathing problem was really getting to be quite restrictive for her.

She always tried to make things as easy for us as she could. She called back one day in March after she had excused herself from the phone on our daily morning call. She said, "Mom, I couldn't talk to you when you called earlier, since we had people here delivering oxygen." Again I had that sinking feeling in my heart and again I couldn't fix it. She said the doctor wanted her to use the oxygen all the time.

A few days passed, and even with the oxygen, her breathing was very difficult. On March 15, Michael and I drove down to see her. We had a good visit and she still looked fairly well. Her color was still good and her eyes remained bright. We spent a few hours with them. Theresa and I talked about when I would come down on March 26. We were both looking forward to the time together.

The morning of March 22, she called me. She was having such a hard time breathing while talking. I said, "Theresa, please don't go downstairs today, it's not worth it. Just stay in bed and rest." She said she would. I said, "I won't keep you on the phone" and I ended our conversation with my daily "I love you" and she replied with her daily "I love you, too." Those would be our last words to each other.

I went to Mass that morning, as had been my daily custom whenever I was able.

I was so distressed about Theresa's breathing. I just prayed to God that if she was ever to be cured, please let the turnaround begin on Good Friday. As I told you in the beginning, on Good Friday of April 1962 she came to us. I then prayed that if she would not be cured, that He please "Take her home."

That afternoon Gerald admitted Theresa to the John Dempsey Hospital, the University Health Center of Connecticut. He called me later and said she was doing better and that her vital signs were good.

At 9:40 that night when I spoke with him she was still doing allright. Then at 10:00 p.m. Gerald called and said that the doctor had called him and told him that he (Gerald) must make a decision to put Theresa on life support or not. He said, "Mom, what should I do?" I said, "Gerald, I don't know if the two of you have discussed it but Theresa and I discussed it in New York. She had said she wanted no life supports and no resuscitation." He then said, "Then you think we should leave it in God's hands?" I said, "Absolutely." He said "Thank you. I love you Mom. I'll keep you posted," and he hung up.

He called us at 4:30 a.m. to tell us that Theresa was gone. How I wanted to put my arms around him. I told him we would be there later that day.

I went to my kitchen window and I looked up at the sky and there was but one beautifully shining star, just one, and it was as if it was Theresa saying, "Here I am, Mom, up here and I'm fine."

My prayer of March 22, at the 9:00 a.m. mass had been answered. On March 23, on Palm Sunday, at 4:00 a.m., He took her home. It had been exactly two years since the date of her original diagnosis. It was the beginning of Holy Week 1997. She left us.

On March 26, the same day I was going to start taking care of her, we laid our beautiful daughter to rest.

This has been the story of our unique child, Theresa. She had evolved from a "rosebud" in her infancy to a "Most Beautiful Rose" in her womanhood.

She was a wife, a mother, a daughter, a sister, a granddaughter, a friend, and now I'm sure she is an angel, a very special angel.

Theresa, I love you still, I always will.

Mom

ABOUT THE AUTHOR

Nancy Moore is not an author by profession, but rather a writer through inspiration.

She is a wife and mother who, along with her husband, was able to share the joy of having been blessed with two wonderful children, their son Michael and their daughter Theresa.

It is about Theresa that this book is written. She is now gone from this earthly dwelling place, but her essence is forever with us. Nancy Moore feels that her spirit can be a beacon of light to all that meet her through this writing of love.